SECRET CODES 2002

DREAMCAST®

GAME BOY® ADVANCE

GAME BOY® COLOR

GAMECUBE™

NINTENDO 64®

PLAYSTATION®

PLAYSTATION® 2

XBOX™

||||||BRADYGAMES
TAKE YOUR GAME FURTHER™

SECRET CODES 2002

BRADYGAMES STAFF

Publisher
David Waybright

Editor-In-Chief
H. Leigh Davis

Marketing Manager
Janet Eshenour

Creative Director
Robin Lasek

Assistant Licensing Manager
Mike Degler

Assistant Marketing Manager
Susie Nieman

CREDITS

Title Manager
Tim Fitzpatrick

Screenshot and Secret Codes Editor
Michael Owen

Book Designer
Kurt Owens

Production Designer
Tracy Wehmeyer

TABLE OF CONTENTS

DREAMCAST® CODES

GAME BOY® ADVANCE CODES

TABLE OF CONTENTS

GAME BOY® ADVANCE CODES cont.

TABLE OF CONTENTS

GAME BOY® COLOR CODES

TABLE OF CONTENTS

GAME BOY® COLOR CODES cont.

TABLE OF CONTENTS

GAMECUBE™ CODES

NINTENDO 64® CODES

TABLE OF CONTENTS

PLAYSTATION® CODES

TABLE OF CONTENTS

PLAYSTATION® 2 CODES

TABLE OF CONTENTS

PLAYSTATION® 2 CODES cont.

XBOX™ CODES

THE GAMES

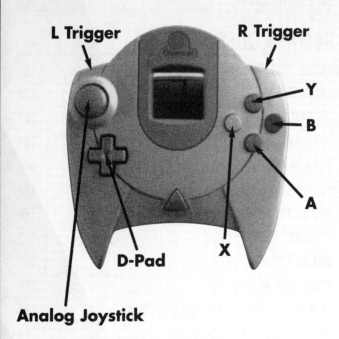

L Trigger

R Trigger

Y

B

A

D-Pad

X

Analog Joystick

ALIEN FRONT ONLINE

FOG MODE

Start an online game called FOGFOGFOG.

BANGAI-O

HIDDEN OPTIONS

Enter the name as 3 Groundhogs. You will find the hidden options under Secret Garden in the options menu.

CRAZY TAXI 2

NO ARROWS

Hold Start as the character select appears and press A.

No Arrows

NO DESTINATION MARK

Hold Y as the character select appears and press A.

EXPERT MODE

Hold Y + Start as the character select appears and press A.

Expert Mode

ALTERNATE VIEW

With controller C Hold Start and press A, B, X or Y to change the view.

Alternate View

CHANGE ARROW COLOR:

With controller C press L.

Change Arrow Color

DAVE MIRRA FREESTYLE BMX

Enter PROQUEST mode to enter the following codes:

UNLOCK SLIM JIM

While in the Rider Select Screen, enter:

Down, Down, Left, Right, Up, Up, Y

Unlock Slim Jim

UNLOCK ALL BIKES

While in the Bike Select Screen, enter:

Up, Left, Up, Down, Up, Right, Left, Right, Y

You will have to perform this code for each of the riders.

Unlock All Bikes

UNLOCK ALL STYLES

While in the Style Selection Screen, enter:

Left, Up, Right, Down, Left, Down, Right, Up, Left, Y

You will have to perform this code for each of the riders.

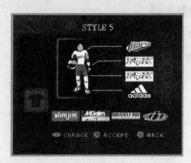

Unlock All Styles

UNLOCK ALL LEVELS

While in the Track Select Screen, enter:

Left, Up, Right, Down, Left, Down, Right, Up, Left, Y

You will have to perform this code for each of the riders.

MAT HOFFMAN'S PRO BMX

X10 SCORE
Pause the game, hold L and press X, B, B, Up, Down, Down.

DIVIDE SCORE BY 10
Pause the game, hold L and press Up, Down, Up, B, B, X.

PERFECT BALANCE
Pause the game, hold L and press X, Left, Up Right.

BALANCE METER
Pause the game, hold L and press Left, B, X, Y, X, B, A.

BIG TIRES
Pause the game, hold L and press Down, B, B, Down.

JUMP HIGHER
Pause the game, hold L and press Up, Up, Up, Up.

UNLIMITED SPECIAL
Pause the game, hold L and press Left, Down, Y, B, Up, Left, Y, X.

SLOW DOWN TIME
Pause the game, hold L and press X, Y, B, A.

MORE TIME
Pause the game, hold L and press X, Up, B, A.

ALTERNATE COLORS
Pause the game, hold L and press Down, Down, Down, Down.

GRANNY
During Career Mode retry any level 10 times in a row.

NBA 2K2

HIDDEN TEAMS

Enter vc as a code.

Hidden Teams

GIANT HEADS

Enter heliumbrain as a code.

MONSTER PLAYERS

Enter alienbrain as a code.

Giant Heads, Monster Players

COMMENTATORS GO BAD...

Enter whatamisaying as a code.

BALL CAMERA

Enter betheball as a code.

Ball Camera

COOL LOOKS

Enter radical as a code.

HIP CLOTHES

Enter the70slive as a code.

WE'RE VERY HAPPY

Enter sohappy as a code.

Extra Player

INFECTED PLAYERS

Enter tvirus as a code.

WE'RE SCREWED EXTRA PLAYER

With the Hidden Teams code enabled, enter Marrinson as a code.

I AM SEAMAN EXTRA PLAYER

With the Hidden Teams code enabled, enter Aynaga as a code.

Extra Player

OOGA BOOGA

MASTER CODE

Select Codes from the options menu and enter IGOTNOSKILLZ.

ALL TRIBAL MISSIONS

Select Codes from the options menu and enter IMINFRANCE.

BOARS

Select Codes from the options menu and enter PORKCHOP.

TIKIS

Select Codes from the options menu and enter IDOLATRY.

BIRDS

Select Codes from the options menu and enter AVIARY.

PLAY AS ABE

Select Codes from the options menu and enter AHOUSEDIVIDED .

PLAY AS DEATH

Select Codes from the options menu and enter SALMONMOUSE.

PLAY AS DISCODUDE

Select Codes from the options menu and enter DOTHEHUSTLE.

PLAY AS DWARF

Select Codes from the options menu and enter HEIGHTCHALLENGED.

PLAY AS LEPRECHAUN

Select Codes from the options menu and enter BLARNEYSTONE.

PLAY AS PIRATE

Select Codes from the options menu and enter WAREZWRONG.

PLAY AS SUPERGUY

Select Codes from the options menu and enter SECRETIDENTITY.

FIREBALL SPELL

Select Codes from the options menu and enter STRIKEAMATCH.

HOMING HEAD SPELL

Select Codes from the options menu and enter DODGETHIS.

LIGHTNING BOLT SPELL

Select Codes from the options menu and enter KILOWATTS.

LIGHTNING CLOUD SPELL

Select Codes from the options menu and enter STORMYWEATHER.

MINE SPELL

Select Codes from the options menu and enter KABOOM.

TORNADO SPELL

Select Codes from the options menu and enter BLOWHARD.

LEVEL 2 MASKS

Select Codes from the options menu and enter ICHEAT.

LEVEL 3 MASKS

Select Codes from the options menu and enter THEREFOREIAM.

LEVEL 4 MASKS

Select Codes from the options menu and enter SOVERYVERY.

LEVEL 5 MASKS

Select Codes from the options menu and enter WEAKANDSAD.

BOAR POLO MODE

Select Codes from the options menu and enter TRICKSHOT.

BOAR RODEO MODE

Select Codes from the options menu and enter SADDLEUP.

TRIBAL TRIAL MOVIE

Select Codes from the options menu and enter STRENGTHNO.

PHANTASY STAR ONLINE

Start a new game. While in the character creation mode, enter the following secret codes as your name to gain additional costumes. After the codes are entered, you can rename yourself as you wish. A happy sound will be played if you entered the code correctly.

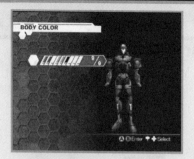

UNLOCK ALTERNATE COSTUMES

EFFECT	CODE
Formarl:	DNEAOHUHEK
Fonewearl:	XSYGSSHEOH
Fonewm:	ASUEBHEBUI
Hucast:	RUUHANGBRT
Humar:	KSKAUDONSU
Hunewearl:	MOEUEOSRHUN
Racaseal:	NUDNAFJOOH
Racat:	MEIAUGHYSN
Ramar:	SOUDEGMKSG

RAINBOW SIX: ROGUE SPEAR

CHEAT MENU

During a game hold A + B + X + Y + L and press Down.

RAZOR FREESTYLE SCOOTER

ALL CHARACTERS AND LEVELS

Pause the game, hold L and press Right, Down, Right, Left, Right, Up, Right, Right.

All Characters

DARYL

Pause the game and press Left, Down, Left, Down, Right, Up, Right, Up.

Daryl

HECTOR

Pause the game and press Left (x5), Right, Left, Right.

Hector

BRITTANY

Pause the game and press Right, Left, Right, Right, Left, Right (x3).

Brittany

TITO ORTIZ

Pause the game and press Down, Up, Right, Down, Up, Left, Down, Up.

Tito Ortiz

CHIPPIE

Pause the game and press Up, Down, Down, Left, Right (x3), Down.

Chippie

TIKIMAN

Pause the game and press Left, Down, Up, Left, Right, Up, Down, Left.

Tikiman

NORTON

Pause the game and press Left, Right, Up, X, Y, X, Up, Right.

Norton

TONY HAWK'S PRO SKATER 2

The following secret codes should be entered at the pause screen while in a game. **Hold the Left Trigger while entering the code.** If the code is entered correctly, you will see the Pause Menu shake.

For secret codes that effect gameplay by altering the environment or the skater, you can disable the option by re-entering the code. For example, if you enter the code for $5000, it won't take the money away again after you re-enter the code.

ENVIRONMENTAL EFFECTS

DISCO LIGHTS
DOWN, UP, X, B, UP, LEFT, UP, A

MOON PHYSICS
A, X, LEFT, UP, DOWN, UP, X, Y

DOUBLE MOON PHYSICS
LEFT, UP, LEFT, UP, DOWN, UP, X, Y, LEFT, UP, LEFT, UP, DOWN, UP, X, Y.

JET PACK MODE
UP, UP, UP, UP, A, X, UP, UP, UP, UP, A, X, UP, UP, UP, UP

Controls:

A = Jet Blast on or off

Y = Hover

L = Strafe left

R = Strafe right

Jet Pack Mode

PERFECT BALANCE
RIGHT, UP, LEFT, X, RIGHT, UP, X, Y

KID MODE
B, UP, UP, LEFT, LEFT, B, UP, DOWN, X

Kid Mode

MIRROR MODE
UP, DOWN, LEFT, RIGHT, Y, A, X, B, UP, DOWN, LEFT, RIGHT, Y, A, X, B

SIM MODE
B, RIGHT, UP, LEFT, Y, B, RIGHT, UP, DOWN

SLO-NIC MODE
B, UP, Y, X, A, Y, B

BLOOD OR NO BLOOD
RIGHT, UP, X, Y

SMOOTH SHADING
DOWN, DOWN, UP, X, Y, UP, RIGHT

Smooth Shading

WIREFRAME MODE
DOWN, B, RIGHT, UP, X, Y

Wireframe Mode

FASTER SPEED
DOWN, X, Y, RIGHT, UP, B, DOWN, X, Y, RIGHT, UP, B

CAREER ENHANCEMENT

INSTANT $5000
A, DOWN, LEFT, RIGHT, DOWN, LEFT, RIGHT

100,000 POINTS IN COMPETITION
X, B, RIGHT, X, B, RIGHT, X, B, RIGHT

CLEAR ENTIRE GAME WITH CURRENT SKATER
B, LEFT, UP, RIGHT, B, LEFT, UP, RIGHT, A, B, LEFT, UP, RIGHT, B, LEFT, UP, RIGHT

SKIP TO RESTART
X, Y, RIGHT, UP, DOWN, UP, LEFT, X, Y, RIGHT, UP, DOWN, UP, LEFT, B, UP, LEFT, Y

STATS

STATS AT 5
UP, X, Y, UP, DOWN

STATS AT 6
DOWN, X, Y, UP, DOWN

STATS AT 7
LEFT, X, Y, UP, DOWN

STATS AT 8
RIGHT, X, Y, UP, DOWN

STATS AT 9
B, X, Y, UP, DOWN

STATS AT 10
A, Y, B, X, Y, UP, DOWN

STATS AT 13
A, Y, B, A, A, A, X, Y, UP, DOWN

UNLOCK CODES

UNLOCK ALL GAPS
DOWN, UP, LEFT, LEFT, B, LEFT, UP, Y, Y, UP, RIGHT, X, X, UP, A

Trixie will become available to you in the character select screen.

Unlock All Gaps

UNLOCK ALL SECRET CHARACTERS

X, B, RIGHT, Y, B, RIGHT, B, Y, RIGHT, X, RIGHT, UP, UP, LEFT, UP, X

UNLOCK EVERY LEVEL

UP, Y, RIGHT, UP, X, Y, RIGHT UP, LEFT, X, X, UP, B, B, UP, RIGHT

UNLOCK EVERYTHING (MASTER CODE!)

This code won't unlock Trixie. You will have to earn her by finding all the gaps or unlocking them all with a code.

A, A, A, X, Y, UP, DOWN, LEFT, UP, X, Y, A, Y, B, A, Y, B.

Once this is entered, end your run.

UNLOCK GYMNASIUM IN SCHOOL LEVEL

Grind the Roll Call! Opunsezmee Rail with about 1:40 on the clock to open the door to the gym.

THE GAMES

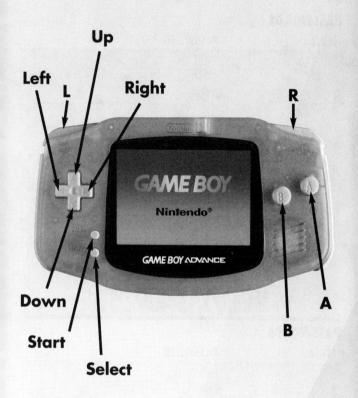

Up

Left

L

Right

R

Down

Start

Select

A

B

ARMY MEN ADVANCE

ALL LEVELS

Enter NQRDGTPB as a password.

PASSWORDS

LEVEL	PASSWORD
2	HJRDCHMC
3	GGRSGJMC
4	FSRSMKMC
5	DQRNBBMC
6	CSRJGCMC
7	BQRDMDPC
8	TJRDQFPC
9	SGRSCQPC
10	RJRNLRPC
11	QGRNRSPC
12	PSRJCTPC

ATLANTIS: THE LOST EMPIRE

PASSWORDS

LEVEL	PASSWORD
2	BMQDNPJS
3	BRZSGZDY

Level 3

4	BVMJFYLG
5	B7JHPMHC
6	C6XQLVNF

Level 6

BACKTRACK

ALL WEAPONS

During a game press Select, then press L, RIGHT, B, L, R, LEFT. Now enter WEAP as a password.

All Weapons

AUTO AMMO

During a game press Select, then press L, RIGHT, B, L, R, LEFT. Now enter AMMO as a password.

INVINCIBILITY

During a game press Select, then press L, RIGHT, B, L, R, LEFT. Now enter GOD as a password.

Auto Ammo

BATMAN: VENGEANCE

PASSWORDS

LEVEL	PASSWORD
2	GOTHAM

Gotham

3	BATMAN
4	BRUCE
5	WAYNE
6	ROBIN
7	DRAKE
8	BULLOCK
9	GRAYSON
10	KYLE
11	BATARANG
12	GORDON
13	CATWOMAN
14	BATGIRL
15	ALFRED

Alfred

BOXING FEVER

PASSWORDS

COMPLETE	PASSWORD
Amateur Series	90HG6738

Amateur Series

Top Contender Series	H7649DH5
Pro Am Series	2GG48HD9
Professional Series	8G3D97B7
World Title	B3G58318
Survival Mode	G51FF888

Survival Mode

CASTLEVANIA: CIRCLE OF THE MOON

MAGICIAN MODE

Complete the game. Start a new game and enter **FIREBALL** as the name.

FIGHTER MODE

Complete the game in Magician mode. Start a new game and enter **GRADIUS** as the name.

SHOOTER MODE

Complete the game in Fighter mode. Start a new game and enter **CROSSBOW** as the name.

Shooter Mode

THIEF MODE

Complete the game in Shooter mode. Start a new game and enter **DAGGER** as the name.

EARTHWORM JIM

LEVEL SELECT

Pause the game and press **Right, R, B, A, L, L, A, R.**

LEVEL CODES

Pause the game and enter the following to skip to that level:

LEVEL	CODE
Buttville	L, A, Up, R, A, R, A, SELECT
Down the Tubes	Up, L, Down, A, R, A
For Pete's Sake	R, L, R, L, A, R
Level 5	R, L, A, B, B, A, L, R
Snot a Problem	R, Up, SELECT, L, R, Left
What the Heck	SELECT, R, B, Down, L, B

F-14 TOMCAT

LEVEL	NOVICE	ACE
2	DHGJKLFF	XDFTRLFF
3	GSDFBFPT	KJTRDBPT
4	RRHCFDVM	RVBPZJVM
5	BPSXFDNF	BMNQYLNF
6	LDFSDTKQ	LFMSDNBQ
7	PXSBSZNJ	PGHPCZNJ
8	DKXZGZQK	DKDGBPQK
9	GKQBGHCT	GSYPZLCT
10	DTRHRPFJ	DCZXRPQR
11	WZPKJYZX	WRTNJYSX
12	JDZFLKFV	JDPQMLRT
13	SPNGDRRG	SPBXBMRG
14	SFGFJHDH	SPXPRGDH
15	LPFHPRFZ	LPFGNBGZ
16	TDKZXSHX	TQWJGZHN
17	DGBVKMNB	BGJKSZPQ
18	KJHGRJCB	PLMNHRTY
19	VBMQRWTP	GLMRTRRC
20	LKFDSPBV	NHDJPBCX

Level 20

21	NHDCDKPM	LCMLFLTC

FIREPRO WRESTLING

EXTRA WRESTLERS

Select **Edit/Edit Wrestler** then select **Name Entry**. Enter **ALL** in the first line. Use the R and L buttons to move between lines. Enter **STYLE** on the left side of the second line and **CLEAR** on the right. Set Exchange to Off and Middle to the Square—this is the default. Press **START** and then back up to the main menu. All of the wrestlers should now be selectable.

Extra Wrestlers

GRADIUS GALAXIES

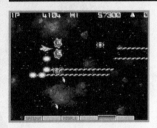

All Weapons

ALL WEAPONS

Pause the game and press UP, UP, DOWN, DOWN, L, R, L, R, B, A.

FAKE KONAMI CODE

Pause the game and press Up, Up, Down, Down, Left, Right, Left, Right, B, A. This will give you all weapons. But shortly after entering the code your ship will be destroyed.

GT ADVANCE CHAMPIONSHIP RACING

EXTRA MODE 1 (MINI CARS)

At the title screen, hold **L + R** and press **Right + B**.

EXTRA MODE 2 (F1 CAR)

At the title screen, hold **L + R** and press **Left + B**.

CREDITS

At the title screen, hold **L + R** and press **Up + B**.

ALL TRACKS

At the title screen, hold **L + R** and press **Up/Right + B**.

ALL CARS

At the title screen, hold **L + R** and press **Up/Left + B**.

ALL TUNE UPS

At the title screen, hold **L + R** and press **Down/Right + B**.

IRIDION 3D

All Levels

ALL LEVELS

Enter ***SH0WT1M3*** as a password.

GALLERY OF RENDERS

Enter ***G4LL3RY*** as a password.

Gallery

PASSWORDS

STAGE	PASSWORD
2	BKMBVNG7L
3	BVOBBFGCH
4	D9DCBYZ7C
5	OLVCVYQGD

Continued

STAGE	PASSWORD
6	8M9CVYV3D
7	XVPDBP6FF

Stage 7

JURASSIC PARK 3: PARK BUILDER

NO DINOSAUR DNA

Enter Zero-Park as a park name.

99,000,000 G

Enter Bonus-Park as a park name.

START WITH ALL SHOP ITEMS

Enter Items-Park as a park name.

99,000,000 G

All Shop Items

HIGH OPINION FROM MEN

Enter Men's-Park as a park name.

HIGH OPINION FROM COUPLES

Enter Love-Park as a park name.

LEGO BIONICLE

MINI-GAMES

Defeat the game with a character to get that character's mini-game.
Alternatively, enter the following code as your name:

CHARACTER	CODE
Gali	9MA268

Gali

Lewa	3LT154
Onua	8MR472
Kopaka	V33673
Pohatu	5MG834
Tahu	4CR487

Tahu

MEN IN BLACK: THE SERIES

PASSWORDS

EPISODE	PASSWORD
3: Alien Technology Lab	HSDSHSBS
4: Rocket Silo	MXNMSNNG
5: MIB Safe House	THXBXSCK

Alien Technology Lab

6: Halloween In Manhattan	NNTNDWNY
End	NFNTMMDD

MONSTERS, INC.

PASSWORDS

DOOR	PASSWORD
3	LRB13G
4	4RB97C
5	7QCZB9

Door 5

NFL BLITZ 20-02

MATCHUP SCREEN CHEATS

Use L, B and A to enter the following codes at the Matchup screen and then press Right.

CODE	EFFECT
432	Infinite Turbo
321	No Random Fumbles
313	Shadow Players
132	Ogre Field
225	Snow Field

PAC-MAN COLLECTION

APPENDIX FOR PAC-ATTACK

From the main menu, select Pac-Attack. Highlight Puzzle, hold Right and press A.

Pac Attack

PAC ATTACK PASSWORDS

LEVEL	PASSWORD
1	STR
2	HNM
3	KST
4	TRT
5	MYX
6	KHL
7	RTS

Continued

LEVEL	PASSWORD
8	SKB
9	HNT
10	SRY
11	YSK
12	RCF
13	HSM
14	PWW
15	MTN
16	TKY
17	RGH
18	TNS
19	YKM
20	MWS
21	KTY
22	TYK
23	SMM
24	NFL
25	SRT
26	KKT
27	MDD
28	CWD
29	DRC
30	WHT
31	FLT
32	SKM
33	QTN

Level 33

LEVEL	PASSWORD
34	SMN
35	TGR
36	WKR
37	YYP
38	SLS
39	THD
40	RMN
41	CNK
42	FRB
43	MLR
44	FRP
45	SDB
46	BQJ
47	VSM
48	RDY
49	XPL
50	WLC
51	TMF
52	QNS
53	GWR
54	PLT
55	KRW
56	HRC
57	RPN
58	CNT
59	BTT
60	TMP
61	MNS
62	SWD
63	LDM
64	YST
65	QTM
66	BRP
67	MRS

Continued

LEVEL	PASSWORD
68	PPS
69	SWT
70	WTM
71	FST
72	SLW
73	XWF
74	RGJ
75	SNC
76	BKP
77	CRN
78	XNT
79	RNT
80	BSK
81	JWK
82	GSN
83	MMT
84	DNK
85	HPN
86	DCR
87	BNS
88	SDC
89	MRH
90	BTF
91	NSM
92	QYZ
93	KTT
94	FGS
96	YLW
97	PNN
98	SPR
99	CHB
100	LST

Level 100

PITFALL: THE MAYAN ADVENTURE

ALL LEVELS, ALL WEAPONS, MOVE ANYWHERE

At the title screen, press **L, SELECT, A, SELECT, R, A, L, SELECT**.

Use **SELECT** and **R or L** to highlight a level. Press **Left** to choose that level.

Hold **SELECT** and press the **B Button** during a game to get 99 of each weapon.

Hold **SELECT** and press in any direction during a game to move in that direction.

START AT LAKAMUL RAIN FOREST

Press **A, L, A, R, A, L, SELECT, SELECT, START** at the title screen.

9 CONTINUES

At the continue screen, repeatedly press **START**.

POWER RANGERS: TIME FORCE

FINAL BATTLE

Enter 8QSD as a password.

Final Battle

RAYMAN ADVANCE

99 LIVES

Pause the game and press Left, Right, Down, Right, Left, R.

ALL MOVES

Pause the game and press Down, Left, Right, Left, Up, L.

INVINCIBILITY

Pause the game and press Right, Up, Right, Left, Right, R.

FULL HEALTH

Pause the game and press L, Down, Left, Up, Down, R.

99 Lives

All Moves

READY 2 RUMBLE BOXING ROUND 2

MICHAEL JACKSON

At the main menu highlight Arcade and press Left, Left, Right, Right, Left, Right, L + R.

Michael Jackson

RUMBLEMAN

At the main menu highlight Championship and press Left, Left, Right, Left, Right, Right, Left, Right, Left, L + R.

Rumbleman

SHAQ

At the main menu highlight Survival and press Left (x4), Right, Right, Left, Left, Right, L + R.

Shaq

ROCKET POWER: DREAM SCHEME

STATUS	PASSWORD
After Ocean Shores Beach	4GWD!KL1

After Ocean Shores

Mad Town Complete	MFKGTB!R
Elementary School Complete	2V74BFDG
Town Square Complete	6!LN99V5
Neighborhood Complete	?FXX6BLJ
Spooky Woods Complete	2L!DZHS8

Spooky Woods

RUGRATS: CASTLE CAPERS

LEVEL	PASSWORD
2	QGPCJNWXGWCB
3	QQTKJYWLGKGF
4	CTKLJKGLSCQR
5	RLPTKKGLWKWP
6	FZLDVHMMDQRB
End	JSJRJKSLXCFJ

End

SPIDER-MAN: MYSTERIO'S MENACE

PASSWORD	BONUS
W7HV1	Fluid Upgrade + Armor Upgrade + Hammerhead Down + Docks and Factory open

W7HV1

| W7HZZ | As above + Web Compressor |
| W7OZZ | As above + Big Wheel Down + Chemcorp open |

Continued

PASSWORD	BONUS
080ZG	As above + Left Wrist Container
Z70Zk	As above + Heavy Impact
Z787k	As above + Rhino Down + Museum Open
ZV87k	As above + Scorpion Down + Right Wrist Container
ZV7Z2	As above + Fire Suit
ZV3Z0	As above + Electric Suit
HV37k	As above + Electro Down + Amusement Park Open
JV37H	As above + Belt
JV310	As above + Symbiote Suit
JV31-	As above + Mysterio Defeated

JV31

SPYRO: SEASON OF ICE

Enter the secret codes by pressing the buttons at the start screen—when Spryo is on screen and "Press Start" is flashing.

UNLOCK SPYRO'S WARP ABILITY

Left, Right, Right, Left, Up, Left, Left, Right, A   (LRRLULLRA)

UNLOCK SPYRO'S WARP ABILITY, UNLOCK ALL LEVELS

Down, Up, Down, Left, Right, Up,, Left, Up, A   (DUDLRULUA)

SPARX GETS 99 LIVES WHEN STARTING A NEW GAME

Left, Right, Right, Right, Down, Up, Right, Up, A   (LRRRDURUA)

INFINITE HEALTH IN SPARX WORLDS

Down, Up, Up, Down, Left, Right, Right, Left, A   (DUUDLRRLA)

INFINITE WEAPONS IN SPARX WORLDS

Down, Right, Up, Left, Left, Up, Right, Down, A   (DRULLURDA)

MORE SPECIAL COMMANDS FOR SPARX

Right, Up, Right, Left, Down, Up, Left, Down, A   (RURLDULDA)

This activates special commands during Sparx worlds, which provides the following controls:

Up + Select	Gives Sparx an Invincibility Shield
Right + Select	Gives Sparx a Smart Bomb
Left + Select	Gives Sparx Rapid Fire
Down + Select	Gives Sparx Homing Bombs
L + Select	Gives Sparx all Keys

OPEN ALL PORTALS TO ALL WORLDS

Up, Up, Down, Down, Left, Right, Up, Down A (UUDDLRUDA)

SUPER STREET FIGHTER 2X REVIVAL

EASIER SPECIAL MOVES

In a single player fight, press Select for easier special moves.

ALTERNATE OUTFIT

Highlight a fighter and press A + B.

RESET

During a game press Select + Start.

TETRIS WORLDS

POPULAR TETRIS

At the Main Menu, highlight Marathon, hold L and press Select. Find the Popular Tetris under the Marathon option.

TONY HAWK'S PRO SKATER

SPIDER-MAN

At the main menu or while paused during a game, hold R and press Up, Up, Down, Down, Left, Right, Left, Right, B, A, START.

SPIDER-MAN WALL CRAWL

At the main menu or while paused during a game, hold R and press Right, A, Down, B, A, START, Down, A, Right, Down. Do a Wall

Spider-Man

Ride and Spidey will continue up the wall. Be careful, this may lock up your GBA!

ALL LEVELS AND MAXIMUM MONEY

At the main menu or while paused during a game, hold R and press B, A, Left, Down, B, Left, Up, B, Up, Left, Left.

ALL LEVELS

At the main menu or while paused during a game, hold R and press A, START, A, Right, Up, Up, Down, Down, Up, Up, Down.

REPLACE BLOOD WITH FACES

At the main menu, hold R and press START, A, Down, B, A, Left, Left, A, Down.

All Levels

Faces

ZOOM IN AND OUT

Pause the game, hold R and press Left, A, START, A, Right, START, Right, Up, START.

ALL CHEATS

At the main menu or while paused during a game, hold R and press B, A, Down, A, START, START, B, A, Right, B, Right, A, Up, Left. You will find the cheats in the Options menu.

All Cheats

NO TIME LEFT

At the main menu or while paused during a game, hold R and press Left, Up, START, Up, Right.

NO BLOOD

At the main menu or while paused during a game, hold R and press B, Left, Up, Down, Left, START, START. Re-enter the code to turn the blood back on.

JET PACK

Pause the game hold R and press Left, A, Start, A, Right, Up, Start. Hold B to fly, L and R to move left and right, and Up and Down to go forward and back.

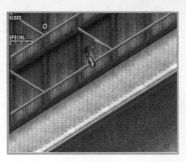

Jet Pack

WILD THORNBERRYS: CHIMP CHASE

LEVEL	PASSWORD
Jungle 2	4S7JXTJ3

Jungle 2

Jungle 3	473H1SZD
Plains 1	B147T3B2
Plains 2	4DZZFB7F
Plains 3	Y5TSGWK2
Arctic 1	6GRHJ74W
Arctic 2	KF3W?6Jr
Arctic 3	MR8594NJ
Outback 1	8!YJCDH4
Outback 2	!!2VKJFS
Outback 3	NDC4SJ3S
Finale	M661M8LB

Finale

THE GAMES

THE GAMES

GAME BOY® COLOR

ABBREVIATION	WHAT IT MEANS
Left	Left on + Control Pad
Right	Right on + Control Pad
Up	Up on + Control Pad
Down	Down on + Control Pad
Start	Press START
Select	Press SELECT
A	Press A Button
B	Press B Button

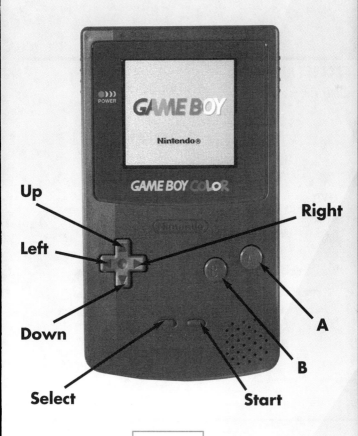

102 DALMATIANS: PUPPIES TO THE RESCUE

GARAGE LEVEL
Enter BONE, BONE, PAWPRINT, TANK as a password.

CAFETERIA LEVEL
Enter DOMINO, BONE, KEY, PAW PRINT as a password.

CRUELLA — FINAL LEVEL
Enter TOY, BONE, BONE, BONE as a password.

ACTION MAN

ACCESS ALL LEVELS
Enter 7!B! as a password.

ATLANTIS: THE LOST EMPIRE

LEVEL	PASSWORD
Submarine	DCNC
Cove	XDKV
Fire	CFCS
Ice	DHCV
Volcano	TJJT
Internal	JMFJ
Palace	QNFS

ARMY MEN 2

PASSWORDS

LEVEL	PASSWORD
1	Mortar, Tank, Mortar, Jeep
2	Jeep, Jeep, Mortar, Plane
3	Tank, Grenade, Tank, Mortar
4	Rifle, Mortar, Jeep, Plane
5	Mortar, Rifle, Plane, Jeep
6	Mortar, Grenade, Rifle, Chopper
7	Plane, Grenade, Rifle, Tank
8	Grenade, Mortar, Chopper, Mortar
9	Tank, Mortar, Rifle, Tank
10	Jeep, Chopper, Tank, Mortar
11	Rifle, Mortar, Grenade, Mortar
12	Jeep, Chopper, Grenade, Chopper
13	Plane, Plane, Grenade, Mortar
14	Plane, Rifle, Plane, Chopper
15	Rifle, Chopper, Chopper, Tank
16	Chopper, Chopper, Rifle, Grenade
17	Rifle, Tank, Plane, Mortar
18	Rifle, Rifle, Grenade, Jeep
19	Rifle, Jeep, Chopper, Grenade
20	Chopper, Grenade, Rifle, Jeep
21	Mortar, Grenade, Chopper, Jeep
22	Rifle, Tank, Chopper, Rifle
23	Plane, Jeep, Tank, Mortar
24	Chopper, Rifle, Jeep, Mortar
25	Tank, Grenade, Plane, Grenade
26	Plane, Tank, Rifle, Mortar
27	Tank, Tank, Jeep, Tank
28	Jeep, Tank, Jeep, Mortar
29	Chopper, Mortar, Chopper, Jeep
30	Tank, Tank, Grenade, Mortar
31	Chopper, Jeep, Grenade, Rifle

ARMY MEN: AIR COMBAT

PASSWORDS

LEVEL	PASSWORD
2	Box, Cross, Box, Box
3	Rocket, Rocket, Rocket, Cross
4	Patch, Rocket, Box, Box
5	Cross, Patch, Cross, Rocket
6	Helmet, Rocket, Patch, Helmet
7	Box, Cross, Rocket, Cross
8	Rocket, Patch, Cross, Helmet
9	Patch, Patch, Rocket, Rocket
10	Cross, Helmet, Cross, Helmet
11	Helmet, Patch, Cross, Helmet
12	Box, Cross, Patch, Patch
13	Rocket, Cross, Helmet, Helmet
14	Patch, Cross, Box, Patch
15	Cross, Box, Patch, Helmet
16	Helmet, Cross, Rocket, Patch

ARMY MEN: SARGE'S HEROES 2

PASSWORDS

LEVEL	PASSWORD
1	P2Z7Q4LB
2	C1F6Q3TP
3	V4R2B1JK
4	X6K2L1KT
5	S5H8L2RG
6	Y2C3T6BF
7	F1C4P9VP
8	VJC2PFHC

LEVEL	PASSWORD
9	W3S4C75S
10	M8R2X4LS
11	KBHD4V1D
12	14NN6168
13	PDO1S4N5
14	B0T7V9CK
15	BDD61977
16	K4TLLC11
17	S6P8D2KG
18	77N5Y14N
19	Y2K4X8TP
20	825VN1N6
21	KFH1JGC0
22	T3F8R0ZY
23	Y7C8R2N0
24	XW3L7B26
25	C2X3Q5TC
26	LV75HRR9
27	D2K7P0S4
28	H4KXJ68D
29	1NSY1912
30	JYMCBB01

BLADE

GAME ENDING

Enter **9?!1N?BKT?51G** as a password.

BUFFY THE VAMPIRE SLAYER

PASSWORDS

LEVEL	PASSWORD
1	3NKFZ8
2	9MD1WV
3	XTN4F7
4	5BVPL2
5	9D6F0S
6	TSCNB4
7	CSJTQZ
8	BNPXZ9

CHICKEN RUN

INVISIBILITY

Enter **Crown, Bronze, Honor, Valor** as a password.

STAGE SKIP

Enter **Honor, Valor, Bronze, Silver** as a password. Pause the game and press **SELECT** to skip to the next stage.

UNLIMITED TIME

Enter **Diamond, Honor, Cross, Crown** as a password.

PASSWORDS

LEVEL	PASSWORD
2	Bronze, Cross, Crown, Bravery
3	Diamond, Bravery, Honor, Bronze
4	Cross, Bravery, Bronze, Bronze
5	Crown, Diamond, Crown, Honor
6	Valor, Diamond, Cross, Silver

DAVE MIRRA FREESTYLE BMX

FULL GAME

Enter **R6KZBS7L1CTQMH** as a password.

Full Game

DEXTER'S LABORATORY: ROBOT RAMPAGE

PLAY AS SUPER ROBOT

At the title screen, press A (x10), B (x10), Select. You will hear a sound if entered correctly.

DONALD DUCK GOIN' QUACKERS

LEVEL	PASSWORD
1-2	YMPHTM9
1-3	VNQJVPY
1-4	2ZSLXSW
1-5	PWYR3XD
2-1	1KC71PL
2-2	53YRKG0
2-3	42XQJJ8

Continued

LEVEL	PASSWORD
2-4	4JD8JK[Diamond]
2-5	6G86G2W
3-1	ZD04XHV
3-2	VO72VCK
3-3	1F871DF

DRIVER

CHEAT MENU

At the Main Menu, highlight Undercover and press Up, Up, Down, Down, Up, Down, Up, Down, Up, Up, Down, Down.

PASSWORDS

LEVEL	PASSWORD
1	Face, Face, Face, Face
2	Tire Mark, Badge, Cone, Red Siren
3	Stop Light, Key, Key, Blue Siren
4	Cone, Cone, Cone, Badge
5	Key, Red Siren, Siren, Stoplight
6	Key, Badge, Tire Mark, Blue Siren
7	Badge, Cone, Badge, Red Siren
8	Red Siren, Badge, Key, Tire Tread
9	Cone, Blue Siren, Red Siren, Red Siren
10	Badge, Badge, Stoplight, Cone
11	Blue Siren, Key, Key, Key
12	Stoplight, Tire Tread, Red Siren, Badge
13	Key, Badge, Badge, Cone
14	Red Siren, Blue Siren, Red Siren, Blue Siren
15	Tire Tread, Key, Cone, Stoplight

M

INSPECTOR GADGET

PASSWORDS

LEVEL	PASSWORD
2	FH2KBH
3	FM!PQM
4	FRVTLR
5	FWQZ!?

JEREMY MCGRATH SUPERCROSS 2000

250CC CLASS

Enter **SHJBBCGB** as a password.

250 CC Class

M & M'S MINIS MADNESS

LEVEL	PASSWORD
1-2	Yellow, Red, Blue, Blue, Green, Blue
1-3	Green, Blue, Yellow, Red, Yellow, Yellow
2-1	Green, Blue, Green, Red, Green, Yellow
2-2	Red, Yellow, Orange, Yellow, Brown, Blue
2-3	Brown, Green, Red, Blue, Orange, Blue

MAT HOFFMAN'S PRO BMX

FINAL STAGE

Enter the password .N.3w.wl2w.

MEN IN BLACK: THE SERIES 2

PASSCODES

LEVEL	PASSCODE
2	MTTH

Level 2

3	STVN
4	SPDM
5	BTHH
6	BBYH
7	MRLL
8	MMDD

Level 8

MONSTERS, INC.

LEVEL	PASSWORD
Himalayas Cave	SN0W
Himalayas Sled	SL3D
Monsters Inc 1	M1K3
Monsters Inc 2	P4PR
Monsters Inc 3	M1NC
Monstropolis Day	D4Y-
Monstropolis Night	N1T3
Scare Floor	BDRM
Secret Lab 1	L4B-
Secret Lab 2	L4BB
Sulley's Apartment	SLLY
The Doorvault	V4LT

MTV SPORTS: T.J. LAVIN'S ULTIMATE BMX

PASSWORDS

LEVEL	PASSWORD
2	VBBCWBBBCX9
3	LBBBHBBBCX9
4	4BBCRBBBCX+
5	GHBFLBBBCX9
6	ZYBBHBCDFX7
7	QHBBNBCGYX5
8	8DVDBBCGYX7
9	DBBDZBCGYX+
10	XZBFWBCGYX4
11	N+BDMBC4YX7

DIRT TRACKS

Enter 6YBBQBBBCBF as a password. You can find the dirt tracks in Practice mode.

THE MUMMY RETURNS

PASSWORDS

LEVEL	PASSWORD
1	71P 4KW
2	8K3 71J
3	P3C 664
4	CXS 0N0
5	1N0 F1N
6	7B4 L6S
7	814 8W4
8	TNM N5Q
9	HTS 0ZX
10	1RD 10V
End	T64 15P

NEW ADVENTURES OF MARY KATE AND ASHLEY

LEVEL PASSWORDS

LEVEL	PASSWORD
Volcano Mystery	CBTHPM
Haunted Camp	GMQTCK
Funhouse Mystery	LHDDQJ
Hotel Who-Done-It	MDGKMQ

PORTAL RUNNER

PASSWORDS

LEVEL	PASSWORD
2	NBNT
3	FDRD
4	NVJV
5	NBRD
6	PDTG
7	NTGT
8	NBGL
9	PDJP
10	NVJC
11	TJDH
12	VLGL
13	TJGL
14	VLJP
15	NTJV
16	NTTG
17	PBRD
18	TCVJ
19	VJDG
20	TGCF
21	NVLC
22	TGCG
23	VJGL
24	PBDP
25	NBDG
26	PDGK
27	PBGR
28	TGKR
29	VJNV
30	TCMT
31	VJRF
32	PCHS

Continued

LEVEL	PASSWORD
33	TGMC
34	VJRJ
35	TGKB
36	NTRJ
End	PDND

POWERPUFF GIRLS: BAD MOJO JOJO

BUTTERCUP GRAPHIC
Enter **CHEMICALX** at the Enter Secrets screen.

BUBBLES GRAPHIC
Enter **BOOGIEMAN** at the Enter Secrets screen.

MAYOR GRAPHIC
Enter **BROCCOLOID** at the Enter Secrets screen.

BOOMER GRAPHIC
Enter **USESNIPS** at the Enter Secrets screen.

BUTCH GRAPHICS
Enter **BESNAILS** at the Enter Secrets screen.

BRICK GRAPHICS
Enter **TAILSRULE** at the Enter Secrets screen.

UNLIMITED SUPER ATTACK
Enter **GIRLPOWER** at the Enter Secrets screen.

UNLIMITED LIVES
Enter **DOGMODE** at the Enter Secrets screen.

UNLIMITED RED CHEMICAL X

Enter **CHERRY** at the Enter Secrets screen.

UNLIMITED BLACK CHEMICAL X

Enter **LICORICE** at the Enter Secrets screen.

UNLIMITED FLIGHT

Enter **IGOTWINGS** at the Enter Secrets screen.

MESSAGE AND PHOTO

Enter **BILLSGIRLS** at the Enter Secrets screen.

ANOTHER MESSAGE AND PHOTO

Enter **RICHARDKIM** at the Enter Secrets screen.

POKEY OAKS SCHOOL LEVEL

Enter **GOGETBUTCH** at the Enter Secrets screen.

ART MUSEUM LEVEL

Enter **DUST BOOMER** at the Enter Secrets screen.

BRICK TRADING CARD

Enter **BESTBUYPWR** or **ZORCH** at the Enter Secrets screen.

PRINCESS TRADING CARD

Enter **SEARS** or **FIZZAT** at the Enter Secrets screen.

POWERPUFF GIRLS TRADING CARD

Enter **CITYRULES** or **TOYSTOWN** at the Enter Secrets screen.

PROFESSOR UTONIUM TRADING CARD

Enter **ANUBISHEAD** or **TARGETGAME** at the Enter Secrets screen.

ROACH COACH TRADING CARD

Enter **ROACHCOACH** at the Enter Secrets screen.

ROWDYRUFF BOYS TRADING CARD

Enter **DOGGIEDO** or **EBWORLD** at the Enter Secrets screen.

SARA BELLUM TRADING CARD

Enter **GAMESTOP** or **SNOWPOKE** at the Enter Secrets screen.

SEDUSA TRADING CARD

Enter **SEDUSA** at the Enter Secrets screen.

UTONIUM CHATEAU TRADING CARD

Enter **TOWNSVILLE** at the Enter Secrets screen.

VOLCANO MOUNTAIN TRADING CARD

Enter **TOYSRUSCOM** at the Enter Secrets screen.

POWERPUFF GIRLS: BATTLE HIM

UNLIMITED RED CHEMICAL X

Enter **CANDYAPPLE** at the Enter Secrets screen.

UNLIMITED BLACK CHEMICAL X

Enter **MIDNIGHT** at the Enter Secrets screen.

UNLIMITED FLIGHT

Enter **JETFUEL** at the Enter Secrets screen.

UNLIMITED LIVES

Enter **UNDEAD** at the Enter Secrets screen.

UNLIMITED SUPER ATTACK

Enter **PHONECARD** at the Enter Secrets screen.

BLOSSOM GRAPHIC

Enter **MISSKEANE** at the Enter Secrets screen.

BUTTERCUP GRAPHIC

Enter **LUMPKINS** at the Enter Secrets screen.

BOOMER GRAPHIC

Enter **WANTSNIPS** at the Enter Secrets screen.

BUTCH GRAPHIC

Enter **SNAILSIAM** at the Enter Secrets screen.

BRICK GRAPHIC

Enter **ITOOKTAILS** at the Enter Secrets screen.

MAYOR GRAPHIC

Enter **MCCRACKEN** at the Enter Secrets screen.

TOWNSVILLE SKIES LEVEL

Enter **GOGETBUTCH** at the Enter Secrets screen.

UTONIUM CHATEAU LEVEL

Enter **BEATBRICK** at the Enter Secrets screen.

MESSAGE AND PHOTO

Enter **BILLSGIRLS** at the Enter Secrets screen.

ANOTHER MESSAGE AND PHOTO

Enter **RICHARDKIM** at the Enter Secrets screen.

ART MUSEUM CARD

Enter **MALPHS** at the Enter Secrets screen.

BOOGIEMAN CARD

Enter **HOTLINE** or **ELBO** at the Enter Secrets screen.

BOOMER CARD

Enter **ICEBREATH** or **BESTBUYHDQ** at the Enter Secrets screen.

CITY OF TOWNSVILLE CARD

Enter **TOYSPOWER** or **TALKINGDOG** at the Enter Secrets screen.

EVIL CAT CARD

Enter **POWERPUFF** at the Enter Secrets screen.

MAYOR CARD

Enter **TOYSTOUGH** or **TARGETPUFF** at the Enter Secrets screen.

RAINBOW THE CLOWN CARD

Enter **MRSBELLUM** or **RICHMONDVA** at the Enter Secrets screen.

TALKING DOG CARD

Enter **BIGBILLY** or **RUFFBOYS** at the Enter Secrets screen.

TOWNSVILLE ART MUSEUM CARD

Enter **MALPHS** at the Enter Secrets screen.

TOWNSVILLE CITY HALL CARD

Enter **PRINCESS** at the Enter Secrets screen.

UTONIUM FAMILY CARD

Enter **FLEETFEET** or **GOTOSEARS** at the Enter Secrets screen.

POWERPUFF GIRLS: PAINT THE TOWNSVILLE GREEN

UNLIMITED RED CHEMICAL X

Enter **RUBIES** at the Enter Secrets screen.

UNLIMITED BLACK CHEMICAL X

Enter **EBONY** at the Enter Secrets screen.

UNLIMITED FLIGHT

Enter **IFLYINSKY** at the Enter Secrets screen.

UNLIMITED LIVES

Enter **QUICKENED** at the Enter Secrets screen.

UNLIMITED SUPER ATTACK

Enter **POWERCALL** at the Enter Secrets screen.

BLOSSOM GRAPHIC

Enter **POKEYOAKS** at the Enter Secrets screen.

BOOMER GRAPHIC

Enter **SNIPSFORME** at the Enter Secrets screen.

BUBBLES GRAPHIC

Enter **UTONIUM** at the Enter Secrets screen.

BUTCH GRAPHIC

Enter **LIKESNAILS** at the Enter Secrets screen.

BRICK GRAPHIC

Enter **GOTMETAILS** at the Enter Secrets screen.

MAYOR GRAPHIC

Enter **OCTIEVIL** at the Enter Secrets screen.

MESSAGE AND PHOTO

Enter **BILLSGIRLS** at the Enter Secrets screen.

ANOTHER MESSAGE AND PHOTO

Enter **RICHARDKIM** at the Enter Secrets screen.

BONSAI GARDEN LEVEL

Enter **DUSTBOOMER** at the Enter Secrets screen.

UTONIUM CHATEAU LEVEL

Enter **BEATBRICK** at the Enter Secrets screen.

ACE CARD

Enter **WUNK** or **GOCIRCUIT** at the Enter Secrets screen.

BIG BILLY CARD

Enter **KABOOM** or **EBSTORE** at the Enter Secrets screen.

BROCCLOID EMPEROR CARD

Enter **MOJOJOJO** at the Enter Secrets screen.

BUTCH CARD

Enter **ROWDYRUFFS** at the Enter Secrets screen.

FUZZY LUMPKINS CARD

Enter **RZONE** at the Enter Secrets screen.

GRUBBER CARD

Enter **TOYSMAGIC** or **GRUBBER** at the Enter Secrets screen.

LITTLE ARTURO CARD

Enter **TOYSCIENCE** or **TARGETPOWR** at the Enter Secrets screen.

MS. KEANE CARD

Enter **FLEETFEET** or **SEARSRULES** at the Enter Secrets screen.

SNAKE CARD

Enter **SQUID** or **BESTBUYPUF** at the Enter Secrets screen.

TOWNSVILLE DUMP CARD

Enter **AMOEBABOYS** at the Enter Secrets screen.

ALL CARDS AND CHEATS

Enter **BILLHUDSON** at the Enter Secrets screen.

POWER RANGERS: TIME FORCE

LEVEL	PASSWORD
2	DBBR
3	GCB5
4	HCB9
End	PB3C or PC3B

RAYMAN

ALL LEVELS PASSWORD

Enter CH5G4mSljD as a password.

ACCESS ALL LEVELS

Pause the game and press A, Left, A, Left, A, B, Right, B, Up, B, A, Left, A, Down, A.

FILL ENERGY

Pause the game and press B, Right, A, Up, B, Left, A, Down, B, Right.

Access All Levels

99 LIVES

Pause the game and press A, Right, B, Up, A, Left, B, Down, A, Right, B, Up, A, Left, B.

99 Lives

ROAD CHAMPS BXS STUNT BIKING

ALL MODES

Enter **QGF7** as a password.

ROCKET POWER: GETTIN' AIR

LEVEL SELECT

DIFFICULTY	PASSWORD
Easy	First Officer, Lars' red-haired friend, Ray, Sam's mom
Medium	First Officer, Lars' red-haired friend, Man with brown hair and glasses, Sam's mom
Hard	First Officer, Lars' red-haired friend, Lar's brown-haired friend, Sam's mom

RUGRATS IN PARIS - THE MOVIE

PASSWORDS

LEVEL	PASSWORD
2	QPRCHJNY
4	ZKHMRTBS

SABRINA THE ANIMATED SERIES: ZAPPED!

PASSWORDS

LEVEL	PASSWORD
1-2	Sabrina, Sabrina, Salem the cat, Jem

Level 1-2

LEVEL	PASSWORD
1-3	Sabrina, Salem the cat, Salem the cat, Red Head Boy
1-4	Sabrina, Harvey, Salem the cat, Harvey
2-1	Salem the cat, Cloey, Sabrina, Salem the cat
2-2	Harvey, Salem the cat, Red Head Boy, Red Head Boy
2-3	Harvey, Harvey, Red Head Boy, Sabrina
2-4	Harvey, Cloey, Red Head Boy, Salem the cat
3-1	Cloey, Jem, Jem, Harvey
3-2	Jem, Harvey, Cloey, Sabrina
3-3	Jem, Cloey, Cloey, Salem the cat
3-4	Jem, Jem, Cloey, Salem the cat
4-1	Red Head Boy, Red Head Boy, Harvey, Cloey
4-2	Sabrina, Cloey, Jem, Salem the cat
4-3	Sabrina, Jem, Jem, Harvey
4-4	Sabrina, Red Head Boy, Jem, Cloey

SCOOBY-DOO!
CLASSIC CREEP CAPERS

PASSWORDS

Select CONTINUE from the main menu and enter the following passwords:

Chapter One: It's A Mystery!

Chapter One

Chapter Two: Boo's Clues!

Chapter Two

Chapter Three: Chemo-Sabotage!

Chapter Three

Chapter Four: Jailbreak!

Chapter Four

Chapter Five: The Plan!

Chapter Five

Chapter Six: Finale!

Chapter Six

SHREK: FAIRY TALE FREAKDOWN

PASSWORDS

STAGE	PASSWORD
Village as Thelonius	LRSVGTLXM
Dungeon as Thelonius	YFSVGTLXK
Village as Shrek	SMHTVKCQR
Dungeon as Shrek	TQDFNHGGM
Swamp as Shrek	TFGKWLSJJ
Dark Forest as Shrek	KDNBQGKVY
Bridge as Shrek	KWJPYXCQC
Castle as Shrek	YNNHLBMBY

SPIDER-MAN 2: THE SINISTER SIX

INVINCIBILITY

At the title screen, press Up, Down, Right, A.

LEVEL SELECT

At the title screen, press B, A, Left, Down, Up, Right.

ONE HIT WITH WEB KILLS

At the title screen, press Down, A, B, A, A.

UNLIMITED WEBS

At the title screen, press Left, Down, B, Up.

TEDDY BEAR MINI GAME

At the title screen, press A, B, A, B, Down.

NIGHTMARE DIFFICULTY

At the title screen, press A, B, Select, Up, Right, Down.

PASSWORDS

STATUS	PASSWORD
Level 2 after defeating Mysterio	MP!63C
Level 3 after defeating Sandman	PL851D
Level 4 after defeating Vulture	MM947F
Level 5 after defeating Scorpion	TS6!96
Level 5-2 after passing the level to fight Kraven	TS6!9G
Level 6 after defeating Kraven	LR6!9G

SPONGEBOB SQUAREPANTS: LEGEND OF THE LOST SPATULA

LEVEL SELECT AND ALL ITEMS

Select CONTINUE and enter D3BVG-M0D3. Pause the game to find a level select.

TONY HAWK'S PRO SKATER 2

ALL BOARDS AND LEVELS

Enter **B58LPT GBBBBV** as a password.

All Boards and Levels

WACKY RACES

ALL DRIVERS AND TRACKS

Enter **MUTTLEY** as a password.

All Drivers and Tracks

WENDY: EVERY WITCH WAY

STATUS	PASSWORD
50% completed	Star, Square, Square, Star
100% completed	Plus, Minus, Plus, Minus

WWF BETRAYAL

DEBUG MODE

Enter 4232 as a password.

X-MEN: MUTANT ACADEMY

APOCALYPSE

Press **Right, Left, Up, Down, Left, Up, B + A** at the title screen.

Apocalypse

Phoenix

PHOENIX

Press **Down, Right, Down, Up, Left, Right, B + A** at the title screen.

X-MEN: MUTANT WARS

PASSWORDS

LEVEL	PASSWORD
2	OKNG6HWB
3	OLNG6HXQ
4	OLNF7HYP

LEVEL	PASSWORD
5	0KPF7HZG
6	1KPF7H0D
7	1KPG7H19
8	1KPF7J2C
9	1KPF7J3L

X-MEN: WOLVERINE'S RAGE

LEVEL PASSWORDS

LEVEL	PASSWORD
2	Wolvie's Mask, Wolvie's Claws, X-Men Insignia, Wolvie's Torso
3	Wolvie's Claws, Sabertooth, Wolvie's Torso, Wolvie's Mask
4	Skull, Wolvie's Mask, X-Men Insignia, Wolvie's Claws
5	Cyber, Lady Deathstrike, Wolvie's Torso, X-Men Insignia
6	Wolvie's Mask, Wolvie's Torso, Wolvie's Head, Lady Deathstrike
7	Wolvie's Claws, Cyber, X-Men Insignia, Skull
8	Skull, X-Men Insignia, Wolvie's Claws, Sabertooth
End	Cyber, Skull, X-Men Insignia, Lady Deathstrike

ALTERNATE COSTUME

At the title screen, press Up, Up, Down, Down, Left, Right, Left, Right, B, A. You'll here Wolverine say, "All Right!"

XTREME SPORTS

CHEAT MENU

At the main menu, press Left (x5), Up (x5), Right (x5), Down (x5), Select (x5).

VIEW CREDITS

Enter your name as "staff" at the Sign-In. Exit the Sign-In and enter the Snack Hut to view the credits.

ALL COMPETITION MEDALS

Enter your name as "xyzzy" at the Sign-In. Exit the Sign-In, hold the A Button and press SELECT. Hold the A Button and press SELECT again to change the Medal count back to zero.

THE GAMES

Control Stick

Y

X

L

R

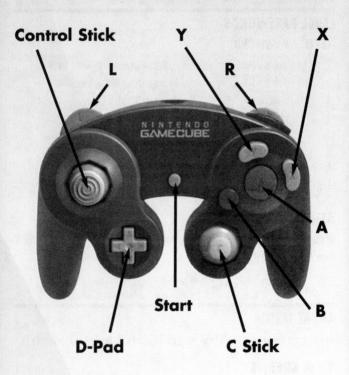

A

Start

B

D-Pad

C Stick

CRAZY TAXI

PUSH BIKE

At the character select, highlight a driver, press L + R, L + R, L + R, then hold L + R + Up and press A.

Push Bike

ANOTHER DAY

At the character select press R and release it. Then hold R and press A.

NO ARROWS

Hold R + Start as the character select appears.

NO DESTINATION MARKERS

Hold L + Start as the character select appears.

EXPERT MODE

Hold L + R + Start as the character select appears and press A.

Expert Mode

NHL HITZ 20-02

CHEATS

After selecting your players, you will have a chance to enter codes by changing three icons with the X Button, Y Button and B Button. Use the X Button to change the first icon, the Y Button for second and the B Button for the third. You will then need to press in the direction indicated. For example, to enter the code for 1st to 7 Wins, you would press X three times, Y two times and B three times. Then press Left on the Directional pad.

EFFECT	CHEAT
Input More Codes	3 3 3 Right
Ignore Last Code	0 1 0 Down
1st to 7 Wins	3 2 3 Left
Win Fights For Goals	2 0 2 Left
No Crowd	2 1 0 Right
Show Hot Spot	2 0 1 Up
Show Shot Speed	1 0 1 Up

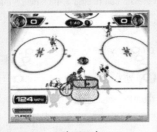

Shot Speed

Rain	1 4 1 Left
Snow	1 2 1 Left
Big Puck	1 2 1 Up
Huge Puck	3 2 1 Up
Bulldozer Puck	2 1 2 Left
Hockey Ball	1 3 3 Left

EFFECT	CHEAT
Tennis Ball	1 3 2 Down

Tennis Ball

No Puck Out of Play	1 1 1 Down
Big Head Player	2 0 0 Right
Huge Head Player	3 0 0 Right

Huge Head Player

Big Head Team	2 2 0 Left
Huge Head Team	3 3 0 Left
Always Big Hits	2 3 4 Down
Late Hits	3 2 1 Down
Pinball Boards	4 2 3 Right
Domino Effect	0 1 2 Right
Turbo Boost	0 0 2 Up
Infinite Turbo	4 1 3 Right
No Fake Shots	4 2 4 Down
No One-Timers	2 1 3 Left
Skills Versus	2 2 2 Down
Hitz Time	1 0 4 Right

THE SIMPSONS: ROAD RAGE

HIDDEN CHARACTERS

Set the system date to the following to open the secret characters:

DATE	CHARACTER
Jan. 1	Happy New Year Krusty the Klown
Oct. 31	Happy Halloween Bart
Nov. 22, 2001, Nov. 28, 2002	Happy Thanksgiving Marge
Dec. 25	Merry Christmas Apu

STAR WARS ROGUE SQUADRON II: ROGUE LEADER

BLACK AND WHITE

Enter LIONHEAD as a password.

The following codes can be found in the Special Features menu after they are entered.

CREDITS

Enter THATSME! as a passcode.

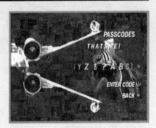

Credits

Art Gallery

MUSIC HALL

Enter COMPOSER as a passcode.

ART GALLERY

Enter EXHIBIT! as a passcode.

AUDIO COMMENTARY

Enter BLAHBLAH as a passcode.

DOCUMENTARY

Enter ?INSIDER as a passcode.

Documentary

TONY HAWK'S PRO SKATER 3

ALL MOVIES

Select Cheats from the Options menu. Enter POPCORN as a code.

All Movies

WAVE RACE: BLUE STORM

PASSWORD SCREEN

At the options menu press X + Z + Start.

Password Screen

DOLPHIN

Enter DLPHNMOD as a password. This will disable the save feature.

Dolphin

GAMES

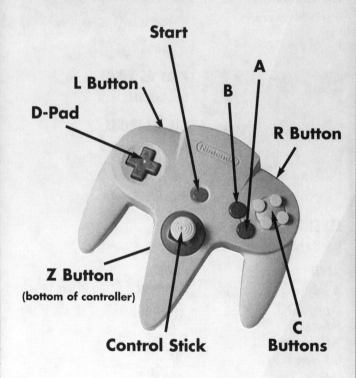

Start

L Button

D-Pad

B

A

R Button

Z Button
(bottom of controller)

C Buttons

Control Stick

ARMY MEN: SARGE'S HEROES 2

PLAY AS PLASTRO

Enter PLSTRLVSVG as a code.

MINI MODE

Enter DRVLLVSMM as a code.

TIN SOLDIER

Enter TNMN as a code.

Tin Soldier

Vikki

PLAY AS VIKKI

Enter GRNGRLRX as a code.

ALL WEAPONS

Enter GBZRK as a code.

MAX AMMO

Enter SLGFST as a code.

LEVEL PASSWORDS

Enter the following as codes to skip to that level:

LEVEL	CODE
2 Bridge	FLLNGDWN
3 Fridge	GTMLK
4 Freezer	CHLLBB
5 Inside Wall	CLSNGN
6 Graveyard	DGTHS
7 Castle	FRNKNSTN
8 Tan Base	BDBZ
9 Revenge	LBBCK

LEVEL	CODE
10 Desk	DSKJB
11 Bed	GTSLP
12 Town	SMLLVLL
13 Cashier	CHRGT
14 Train	NTBRT
15 Rockets	RDGLR
16 Pool	FSTNLS
17 Pinball	WHSWZRD

BANJO-TOOIE

CHEATS

Enter the Code Chamber in Mayahem Temple. Stand on the platform in the center and spell CHEATO to access the code entry session.

Cheats

CODE	EFFECT
JIGGYWIGGYSPECIAL	Level select
SUPERBANJO	Faster Banjo
SUPERBADDY	Faster enemies
GNIMOH	Homing eggs
SREHTAEF	Doubles feather capacity
SGGE	Doubles egg capacity
NESTKING	Infinite feathers and eggs
KCABYENOH	Energy refills

Continued

CODE	EFFECT
FOORPLLAF	No damage from falling
XOBEKUJ	Jukebox at Jolly Roger's Lagoon
YGGIJTEG	Jiggy signs in Jiggywiggy's Temple
PLAYITAGAINSON	All cinemas in Replay Mode
JIGGYSCASTLIST	Character Parade

Character Parade

CONKER'S BAD FUR DAY

From the Cock and Plucker, select Options and then enter Cheats. Now, enter the following codes. The Fire Imp will acknowledge whether you entered a correct cheat or not. Try entering the wrong cheat two times in a row—he'll say something special.

IN-GAME CHEATS

50 LIVES
BOVRILBULLETHOLE

VERY EASY MODE
VERYEASY

EASY MODE
EASY

UNLOCK CHAPTERS IN CHAPTER MODE

UNLOCK BARN BOYS
PRINCEALBERT

NINTENDO 64®   C

UNLOCK BATS TOWER
CLAMPIRATE

UNLOCK SLOPRANOS
ANCHOVYBAY

UNLOCK UGA BUGA
MONKEYSCHIN

UNLOCK SPOOKY
SPANIELSEARS

UNLOCK IT'S WAR
BEELZEBUBSBUM

UNLOCK THE HEIST
CHOCOLATESTARFISH

UNLOCK EVERY CHAPTER AND CUT-SCENE
WELDERSBENCH

MULTIPLAYER CHARACTER CHEATS

UNLOCK CONKER
WELLYTOP

UNLOCK NEO CONKER
EASTEREGGSRUS

UNLOCK GREG THE GRIM REAPER
BILLYMILLROUNDABOUT

UNLOCK SERGEANT AND TEDIZ LEADER
RUSTYSHERIFFSBADGE

UNLOCK ZOMBIES AND VILLAGERS
BEEFCURTAINS

UNLOCK CAVEMAN

EATBOX

UNLOCK WEASEL

CHINDITVICTORY

EXTRA MULTIPLAYER CHEATS

UNLOCK THE FRYING PAN IN THE RACE

DUTCHOVENS

UNLOCK THE BASEBALL BAT IN THE RACE

DRACULASTEABAGS

EXTRA BRUTAL MULTIPLAYER

SPUNKJOCKEY

This is a weird one. Play multiplayer alone in a level that has Katana Swords and Chainsaws. Get one of them and attack the enemy for a cool death animation.

NFL BLITZ 2001

VERSUS CODES

To enter the following codes, the Z Button is for the first slot, A Button is for the second slot and the B Button is the third slot. Then end it with a direction on the Control Stick.

EFFECT	CODE
Tournament mode (in a 2 team game)	1-1-1 Down
Show field goal %	0-0-1 Down
Punt hang time meter	0-0-1 Right
Fast turbo running	0-3-2 Left
Huge head	0-4-0 Up
Super blitzing	0-4-5 Up
Hide receiver name	1-0-2 Right

EFFECT	CODE
Super field goals	1-2-3 Left

Super Field Goals

No punting	1-5-1 Up
No head	3-2-1 Left
Headless team	1-2-3 Right

Headless Team

Big head	2-0-0 Right
Big heads team	2-0-3 Right
Big football	0-5-0 Right
Tiny players team	3-1-0 Right

Tiny Players

Continued

EFFECT	CODE
No first downs	2-1-0 Up
Allow stepping out-of-bounds	2-1-1 Left
Fast passes	2-5-0 Left
Power-up teammates	2-3-3 Up
Power-up offense	3-1-2 Up
Power-up blockers	3-1-2 Left
Power-up defense	4-2-1 Up
Target receiver (no highlighting)	3-2-1 Down
Always QB	2-2-2 Left
Always receiver (requires human teammate)	2-2-2 Right
QB/receiver cancel always	3-3-3 Up
No interceptions	3-4-4 Up
No random fumbles	4-2-3 Down
Invisible (no effect)	4-3-3 Up
Turn off stadium	5-0-0 Left

Turn off Stadium

Weather: clear	2-1-2 Left
Weather: snow	5-2-5 Down

The following codes require both teams to agree (enter the same code):

EFFECT	CODE
Smart CPU	3-1-4 Down
No CPU assistance	0-1-2 Down
Show more field	0-2-1 Right

Show More Field

Power-up speed	4-0-4 Left
No play selection	1-1-5 Left
Super blitzing	0-4-5 Up
Hyper blitz mode	5-5-5 Up

READY 2 RUMBLE BOXING: ROUND 2

MICHAEL JACKSON

Highlight the "Survival" option at the main menu, then press Left (x2), Right (x2), Left, Right, L + R. Alternatively, successfully complete the game in arcade mode two times to unlock Michael Jackson.

SHAQUILLE O'NEAL

Highlight the "Survival" option at the main menu, then press Left (x4), Right (x2), Left (x2), Right, L + R. Alternatively, successfully complete the game in arcade mode five times to unlock Shaquille O'Neal.

ZOMBIE BOXER

Press Left, Up, Right, Down, R (x2), L at the character selection screen.

SCOOBY-DOO! CLASSIC CREEPY CAPERS

UNLIMITED COURAGE

During gameplay as Shaggy hold L and press C-Up, C-Left, C-Down, C-Up, C-Down, Up, Right, Down, Left, Up, Left, Down, Right, Up, Down.

LEVEL SKIP

During gameplay as Shaggy hold L and press C-Up, C-Down, C-Up, C-Down, Up, Down, Up, Down, Left, Right, Left, Right.

TONY HAWK'S PRO SKATER 2

10X POINTS

Pause the game, hold L and press C-Down (x4), C-Left, C-Right, Right.

STATS TO 10

Pause the game, hold L and press Down, Up, C-Up, C-Left, Down, Up, C-Up.

STATS TO 13

Pause the game, hold L and press C-Down, C-Right (x2), C-Up, Up, Down, Right, Left.

JET PACK MODE

Pause the game, hold L and press Right, Up, C-Down, C-Up, C-Down, C-Left, C-Left, C-Right. Ollie to hover.

PERFECT BALANCE

Pause the game, hold L and press C-Down, Right, Down, C-Left, C-Down, C-Up, C-Right, C-Left.

UNLIMITED SPECIAL

Pause the game, hold L and press C-Left, C-Down, C-Up, Right, C-Right, Right.

ALL TAPES

Pause the game, hold L and press C-Right, Left, Up, C-Up (x2), Right, Down, Up.

THIN SKATER

Pause the game, hold L and press Left, C-Right, Right, Down, C-Down, Up, Up. You can repeat this code to make thinner.

TURBO MODE

Pause the game, hold L and press
C-Left, C-Down, C-Up, Down, Up, Right.

SIMULATION MODE

Pause the game, hold L and press Left,
C-Right, Right, Down, C-Down, Up, Up.

MAXIMUM TURBO

Pause the game, hold L and press
Down, Left, C-Up, C-Down, C-Left,
Right, Up.

SKIP TO RESTART

Pause the game, hold L and press
C-Left, C-Down, C-Right, Down,
C-Up, C-Up.

SLOW-NIC MODE

Pause the game, hold L and press
C-Up, Down, Left, C-Left, C-Down, C-Up,
C-Right. Tricks will be in slow motion.

DOUBLE MOON PHYSICS

Pause the game, hold L and press
C-Down, C-Left, C-Right, C-Left, Up,
C-Down, Down, Right, C-Down, C-Down.

WCW BACKSTAGE ASSAULT

ALL HIDDEN WRESTLERS

At the main menu press C-Left, C-Left, C-Right, C-Right, C-Right.

SMALL WRESTLERS

At the main menu press R, R, L, L, C-Left, C-Right.

BIG WOMEN WRESTLERS

At the main menu press R, R, B, B, L, L.

UNLIMITED STAMINA

At the main menu press R, R, B, R, R, B.

INDESTRUCTIBLE WEAPONS

At the main menu press L, R, L, R, C-Left, C-Left.

ALTERNATE GRUNTS

At the main menu press R, L, R, L, B, B.

PLAYSTATION®

THE GAMES

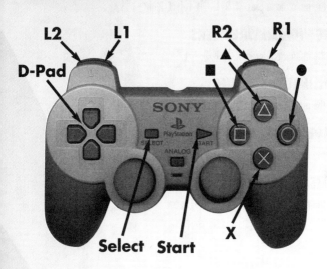

007 RACING

ASTON MARTIN VANTAGE IN TWO-PLAYER

At the title screen, press L1, R1, ▲, ●, X. You'll hear a sound if the codes was entered correctly.

ARMY MEN: AIR ATTACK 2

PASSWORDS

Password Screen

MISSION	PASSWORD
2	Up, X, ▲, Right, Left, ■, ●, X
3	▲, ●, Down, Left, ■, ■, Up, Up
4	X, Right, Left, X, ●, ■, ■, ▲
5	Down, Down, ●, ■, ●, ■, Right, X
6	▲, X, Up, Left, Right, Left, ●, ▲
7	Left, ■, Right, Down, ●, X, X, Right
8	▲, Right, ■, ■, ●, Down, Down, X
9	Up, X, ■, Left, Right, ●, Left, Left
10	▲, Up, ●, X, ■, Down, Down, Down
11	●, ●, Up, Left, Right, X, ▲, ■
13	Left, Left, ▲, ●, X, X, Down, Right
15	Left, Right, ●, X, ■, Down, Down, ●
16	▲, ●, X, Right, Right, ●, ■, Down
18	●, X, Right, ▲, ■, Up, X, X
20	Up, X, ●, Up, Left, ■, ●, X

Continued

MISSION	PASSWORD
21	Left, ●, ▲, Down, X, X, X, ●
22	▲, X, Down, Left, Right, X, ●, ■

Level 22

COOL BOARDERS 2001

UNLOCK EVERYTHING

Select Career Mode and enter your name as GIVEALL.

DAVE MIRRA FREESTYLE BMX

UNLOCK SLIM JIM

At the Rider Select screen, press Down, Down, Left, Right, Up, Up, Circle.

Slim Jim

ALL BIKES

At the Bike Select screen, press Up, Left, Up, Down, Up, Right, Left, Right, Circle.

All Bikes

ALL STYLES

At the Style Select screen, press Left, Up, Right, Down, Left, Down, Right, Up, Left, Circle.

FEAR EFFECT 2: RETRO HELIX

CHEAT MODE

First you must complete the game and start a new game. Once you have control of Hana, you should come to a console. Enter the following codes:

Control of Hana

Console

EFFECT	CODE
Big Head	10397
All Weapons	11692
Infinite Ammo	61166

Big Head

ART GALLERIES

At the title screen, enter the following codes for the respective disc to open the Art Gallery. You can find the Art Gallery in the Extras section of the Options menu.

Art Gallery

DISC	CODE
One	Left, Right, Up, Down, Down, ●
Two	Up, Up, R1, R1, R1, ■
Three	L1, R2, L1, R2, L1, ■
Four	●, ●, ■, L2, ■

Art Gallery

INCREDIBLE CRISIS

CHANGE SIZE OF HEAD

Press Up or Down using the D-Pad of the second controller.

CHANGE SIZE OF CHARACTER

Press Left or Right using the D-Pad of the second controller.

KNOCKOUT KINGS 2001

HIDDEN BOXERS

Enter the following names in the career mode to unlock these hidden boxers:

ENTER THIS NAME	TO OPEN THIS HIDDEN BOXER
100%	Full stats

Full Stats

BABY	Baby

Baby Boxer

BULLDOG	Bulldog

Bow-wow Boxer

ENTER THIS NAME	TO OPEN THIS HIDDEN BOXER
CLOWN	Clown

Bozo Boxer

EYE	One Eye

Cyclops

GORE	Gorilla

Gorilla

NOLAN	Owen Nolan
FRANCIS	Steve Francis

MAT HOFFMAN'S PRO BMX

At the Pause menu (during a session in a level, press Start), hold L1 and enter the following codes.

8 MINUTES ADDED TO YOUR RUN TIME

■, Up, ●, X

Entering the following codes will toggle the cheat on and off.

BIG TIRES

Down, ●, ●, Down

SPECIAL BAR ALWAYS FULL

Left, Down, ▲, ●, Up, Left, ▲, ■

GRIND BALANCE BAR

Left, ●, ■, ▲, ■, ●, X

PERFECT BALANCE

■, Left, Up, Right

ALL SCORES MULTIPLIED BY 10

■, ●, ●, Up, Down, Down

ALL SCORES DIVIDED BY 10

Down, Down, Up, ●, ●, ■

NASCAR 2001

CODES

Enter the Credits menu located in the Options menu and then select Development. Make sure to enter the codes after the movie and during the credits to access the following extras.

ENTER THIS CODE	TO ACCESS
Hold L2 and press ■, ●, ▲, X	Asher Boldt

Asher Boldt

Hold R1 and press ■, ▲, ■, ▲	John Andretti's Spare Car

Andretti's Spare Car

Continued

ENTER THIS CODE	TO ACCESS
Hold L2 and press ■, ●, X, Down, Up, Right, Left	KC Monoxide

KC Monoxide

| Hold R2 and press ■, ●, X, Up, Down, Left, Right | Shorty Leung |

Shorty Leung

| Hold L1 and press ■, ▲, ■, ●, ■, X | Jocko Micaels |

Jocko Micaels

ENTER THIS CODE	TO ACCESS
Hold R1 and press Left, ●, Up, Down, Right, Right, Right	Proving Grounds Track

Proving Grounds

ENTER THIS CODE	TO ACCESS
Hold L2 and press ■, ●, ■, Up, Up, Down, Up, Left, Right, **X**	Treasure Island Track

Treasure Island

NCAA FOOTBALL 2001

CHEAT CODES

Select Game Settings/Secret Codes and enter the following:

EFFECT	CHEAT
Max Recruit Points	HEADCOACH
Maximum Attributes	BALLER
Always Catch Passes	HANDSOFGLUE
Quicker Players	SCRAMBLE
Slow Players	CEMENTFEET

Continued

EFFECT	CHEAT
Defense Always Intercepts	OSKIE
Reveal Plays	MINDREADER
Maximum Wind	SAFTEY
Faster Day to Night	DAYNIGHT
All Stadiums	OPENSESAME
The Juggernaut Team	BULLDOZER
Change Date	Y2K
View the Whole Poll	POPULARITY

NCAA GAMEBREAKER 2001

EASTER EGGS

Select Customize/Easter Eggs and enter the following:

EFFECT	CHEAT
All Blue Chips	MOTIVATE
Player Attributes at 99	BEAT DOWN
Better Walk-on Players	FRANKENSTEIN
Excellent Stats	Vers
Better Running	REAL ESTATE
Better Passing	GO DEEP
Stronger Defense	PHYSICAL
Strong Stiff Arm	HAMMER
Big Team Vs. Small Team	BIGandsmall
Credits	HOLLYWOOD

NFL BLITZ 2001

VS CHEATS

You must enter the following codes at the Versus screen by pressing the Turbo, Jump, and Pass buttons. For example, to get Infinite Turbo press Turbo (x5), Jump (x1), Pass (x4), and then press Up.

EFFECT	CODE
Tournament Mode (2-player game)	1,1,1 Down
Infinite Turbo	5,1,4 Up
Fast Turbo Running	0,3,2 Left
Power-up Offense	3,1,2 Up
Power-up Defense	4,2,1 Up
Power-up Teammates	2,3,3 Up
Power-up Blockers	3,1,2 Left
Super Blitzing	0,4,5 Up
Super Field Goals	1,2,3 Left
Invisible	4,3,3 Up

Invisible

No Random Fumbles	4,2,3 Down
No First Downs	2,1,0 Up
No Interceptions	3,4,4 Up
No Punting	1,5,1 Up
Allow Stepping Out of Bounds	2,1,1 Left
Fast Passes	2,5,0 Left
Late Hits	0,1,0 Up
Show Field Goal %	0,0,1 Down
Show Punt Hangtime Meter	0,0,1 Right

Continued

EFFECT	CODE
Hide Receiver Name	1,0,2 Right
Big Football	0,5,0 Right
Big Head	2,0,0 Right
Huge Head	0,4,0 Up

Huge Head

Team Tiny Players	3,1,0 Right
Team Big Players	1,4,1 Right
Team Big Heads	2,0,3 Right

Team Big Heads

Weather: Snow	5,2,5 Down
Weather: Rain	5,5,5 Right
No Hiliting on Target Receiver	3,2,1 Down
Red, White and Blue Ball	3,2,3 Left
Unlimited Throw Distance	2,2,3 Right
Deranged Blitz Mode (1-player game)	2,1,2 Down
Ultra Hard Mode (1-player game)	3,2,3 Up
Smart CPU Opponent (1-player game)	3,1,4 Down
Always Quarterback	2,2,2 Left

EFFECT	CODE
Always Receiver	2,2,2 Right
Cancel Always Quarterback/Receiver	3,3,3 Up
Show More Field (2-player agreement)	0,2,1 Right
No CPU Assistance (2-player agreement)	0,1,2 Down
Power-up Speed (2-player agreement)	4,0,4 Left
Hyper Blitz (2-player agreement)	5,5,5 Up
No Play Selection (2-player agreement)	1,1,5 Left
Super Passing (2-player agreement)	4,2,3 Right

TEAM PLAYBOOKS

EFFECT	CODE
Arizona Cardinals	1,0,1 Left
Atlanta Falcons	1,0,2 Left
Baltimore Ravens	1,0,3 Left
Buffalo Bills	1,0,4 Left
Carolina Panthers	1,0,5 Left
Chicago Bears	1,1,0 Left
Cincinnati Bengals	1,1,2 Left
Cleveland Browns	1,1,3 Left
Dallas Cowboys	1,1,4 Left
Denver Broncos	1,1,5 Right
Detroit Lions	1,2,1 Left
Green Bay Packers	1,2,2 Left
Indianapolis Colts	1,2,3 Up
Jacksonville Jaguars	1,2,4 Left
Kansas City Chiefs	1,2,5 Left
Miami Dolphins	1,3,1 Left
Minnesota Vikings	1,3,2 Left
New England Patriots	1,3,3 Left
New Orleans Saints	1,3,4 Left
New York Giants	1,3,5 Left
New York Jets	1,4,1 Left
Oakland Raiders	1,4,2 Left
Philadelphia Eagles	1,4,3 Left

Continued

EFFECT	CODE
Pittsburgh Steelers	1,4,4 Left
San Diego Chargers	1,4,5 Left
San Francisco 49ers	1,5,1 Left
Seattle Seahawks	1,5,2 Left
St. Louis Rams	1,5,3 Left
Tampa Bay Buccaneers	1,5,4 Left
Tennessee Titans	1,5,5 Left
Washington Redskins	2,0,1 Left

NFL GAMEDAY 2002

CODES

Select Code Entry from the options and enter the following:

CODE	EFFECT
5280 CLUB	Mile High Stadium

Mile High Stadium

GRUDGE MATCH	GameDay stadium
989 SPORTS	989 team
RED_ZONE	Redzone team

CODE	EFFECT
ALL BOBO	Everyone named Bobo

Everyone named Bobo

BASKETBALL	Players named after NBA players
OVAL OFFICE	Players named after Presidents
EURO LEAGUE	Players named after NFL Europe players
EVEN STEVEN	Even teams
BIG PIG	Big football
TINY	Big players
MUNCHKINS	Small players
PENCILS	Thin and tall
ENDURANCE	More endurance
FATIGUE	Reduce fatigue
MR GLASS	Injured hamstring
MR FURIOUS	Hop-a-long

Hop-a-long

CODE	EFFECT
POP WARNER	Players float

Players Float

LINE BUSTER	Better defensive line
SUPER FOOT	Better Running Back
FASHION SHOW	Cheerleader pictures after the game

Cheerleaders

CREDITS	Credits

Credits

SIMPSONS WRESTLING

ZERO HEALTH LOSSES

At the title screen press ●, R1, R1, R1, Right, Left.

INFINITE ENERGY

At the title screen press ●, R1, R1, R1, Down, Up.

Infinite Energy

Big Ape Arena

MULTI-ROPE ATTACK:

At the title screen press ●, R1, R1, R1, Up, Down.

BIG APE ARENA

At the title screen press ●, R2, R1, ●, R2, R1.

BIG HEAD

At the title screen press ●, L1, L1, L1, Up, Down.

BIG APE MODE

At the title screen press ●, L1, ●, R1, ●, L2, ●.

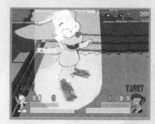

Big Head

Big Ape Mode

NO OUTLINES

At the title screen press ●, Right, Up, Right, Down.

FLAT LAND

At the title screen press ●, L1, L1, L1, Left, Right.

BONUS MATCH

At the title screen press ●, Up, Up, Down, Down, Left, Right, Left, Right. Select Bonus Match Up at the main menu.

Flat Land

Bonus Match

CREDIT GAGS

At the title screen press ●, L1, ●, L1, ●, R1, ●, R1.

MIRROR MATCHES

At the title screen press Up, Up, Down, Down, Left, Right, Left, Right, ●, L2, ●, R2, ●, L1, ●, R1.

BUMBLEBEE MAN

At the title screen press ●, Left, Up, Left, Down, R1.

MOE

At the title screen press ●, Left, Up, Left, Down, L1.

NED FLANDERS

At the title screen press ●, Left, Up, Left, Down, L2.

PROFESSOR FRINK

At the title screen press ●, Left, Up, Left, Down, R2.

DISPLAY COMPLETION DATE

At the title screen press ■, ●, L1, R1.

128

SNO-CROSS CHAMPIONSHIP RACING

These codes should be entered while at the main menu. Hold the R1 button, enter the code and then release the R1 button to finish the code.

RACE ON AN ATV
Up, Right, Down, Up, Right, Down

RACE ON A GOCART
Right, Right, Left, Left, Right, Right

Race on an ATV

UNLOCK SECRET CARTOON TRACK
Right, Up, Left, ●, ▲, ■

Choose the single-player mode and race on the Kiruna Track to see the cartoon landscape.

Race on a GoCart

UNLOCK THE SUMMER TRACK
▲, X, ●, ●, X, ▲

Choose the single-player mode and race on the Calgary Track to race on the dirt track.

Cartoon Track

Summer Track

UNLOCK EVERY LEAGUE, SNOWMOBILE AND TRACK
Up, ▲, Up, ▲, Up, ▲

LAUNCH THE DEMO MODE
Up, Up, Up, Down, Down, Down

SPIDER-MAN 2: ENTER ELECTRO

UNLOCK ALL CHEATS

Select Cheats from the Special Menu and enter AUNTMAY.

UNLOCK COSTUMES

Select Cheats from the Special Menu and enter WASHMCHN.

Unlock Costumes

UNLOCK GALLERY

Select Cheats from the Special Menu and enter DRKROOM.

Unlock Gallery

UNLOCK TRAINING

Select Cheats from the Special Menu and enter CEREBRA.

UNLOCK LEVELS

Select Cheats from the Special Menu and enter NONJYMNT.

BIG FEET

Select Cheats from the Special Menu and enter STACEYD.

Unlock Levels

BIG HEAD

Select Cheats from the Special Menu and enter ALIEN.

Big Head

DEBUG MODE

Select Cheats from the Special Menu and enter DRILHERE.

WHAT IF

Select Cheats from the Special Menu and enter VVISIONS.

VV HIGH SCORES

Select Cheats from the Special Menu and enter VVHISCRS.

High Scores

TONY HAWK'S PRO SKATER 2

NEVERSOFT CHARACTERS

At the Main Menu, hold L1 and press Up, ■, ■, ▲, Right, Up, ●, ▲. This causes the wheel to spin. Then create a skater and give him the name of anyone on the Neversoft team. For example, name your skater Mick West and he'll appear. The best one is Connor Jewett, the son of Neversoft's President. (Don't change the appearance of the kid-sized skaters. It could crash your game.)

You must enter the following codes after pausing the game. While the game is paused, press and hold L1, and enter the codes.

JET PACK MODE

Up, Up, Up, Up, X, ■, Up, Up, Up, Up, X, ■, Up, Up, Up, Up

Hold ▲ to hover

Press X to turn on the Jetpack

Press forward to move forward

FATTER SKATER

X (x4), Left, X (x4), Left, X (x4), Left

Fatter Skater

THINNER SKATER

X (x4), ■, X (x4), ■, X (x4), ■

TOGGLE BLOOD ON/OFF

Right, Up, ■, ▲

SPECIAL METER
ALWAYS YELLOW

X, ▲, ●, ●, Up, Left, ▲, ■

Special Meter

SUPER SPEED MODE

Down, ■, ▲, Right, Up, ●, Down, ■, ▲, Right, Up, ●

UNLOCK EVERYTHING

X, X, X, ■, ▲, Up, Down, Left, Up, ■, ▲, X, ▲, ●, X, ▲, ●

BIG HEAD

■, ●, Up, Left, Left, ■, Right, Up, Left

ALL GAPS

Down, Up, Left, Left, ●, Left, Up, ▲, ▲, Up, Right, ■, ■, Up, X

This will give you Private Carrera.

Big Head

ALL SECRET
CHARACTERS

■, ●, Right, ▲, ●, Right, ●, ▲, Right, ■, Right, Up, Up, Left, Up, ■

MOON PHYSICS

X, ■, Left, Up, Down, Up, ■, ▲

DOUBLE MOON PHYSICS

Left, Up, Left, Up, Down, Up, ■, ▲, Left, Up, Left, Up, Down, Up, ■, ▲

$5000

X, Down, Left, Right, Down, Left, Right

100,000 POINTS IN COMPETITION

■, ●, Right, ■, ●, Right, ■, ●, Right

This will end the competition.

ACCESS ALL LEVELS

Up, ▲, Right, Up, ■, ▲, Right, Up, Left, ■, ■, Up, ●, ●, Up, Right

STATS AT 5

Up, ■, ▲, Up, Down

STATS AT 6

Down, ■, ▲, Up, Down

STATS AT 7

Left, ■, ▲, Up, Down

STATS AT 8

Right, ■, ▲, Up, Down

STATS AT 9

●, ■, ▲, Up, Down

STATS AT 13

X, ▲, ●, X, X, X, ■, ▲, Up, Down

STATS AT ALL 10s

X, ▲, ●, ■, ▲, Up, Down

SKIP TO RESTART

■, ▲, Right, Up, Down, Up, Left, ■, ▲, Right, Up, Down, Up, Left, ●, Up, Left, ▲

CLEAR GAME WITH CURRENT SKATER

●, Left, Up, Right, ●, Left, Up, Right, X, ●, Left, Up, Right, ●, Left, Up, Right

KID MODE
●, Up, Up, Left, Left, ●, Up, Down, ■

MIRROR LEVEL
Up, Down, Left, Right, ▲, X, ■, ●, Up, Down, Left, Right, ▲, X, ■, ●

PERFECT BALANCE
Right, Up, Left, ■, Right, Up, ■, ▲

WIREFRAME
Down, ●, Right, Up, ■, ▲

SLO-NIC MODE
●, Up, ▲, ■, X, ▲, ●

SIM MODE
●, Right, Up, Left, ▲, ●, Right, Up, Down

SMOOTH SHADING
Down, Down, Up, ■, ▲, Up, Right

DISCO LIGHTS
Down, Up, ■, ●, Up, Left, Up, X

X-MEN:
MUTANT ACADEMY 2

UNLOCK EVERYTHING
At the title screen press Select, Down, R2, L1, R1, L2.

Unlock Everything

THE GAMES

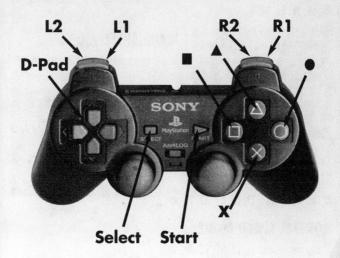

L2   L1

D-Pad

R2   R1

Select   Start

X

4X4 EVOLUTION

ALL TRUCKS

At any menu press L1, L2, R1, R2, L1, R1.
This allows access to the cheat class of Ford
Explorer Sport Tracs.

$1 MILLION IN CAREER MODE

At any menu press L2, ■, R1, ●, R1, L1,
●, L2, ■, R2, ■, R1.

All Trucks

$1 Million in Career

WARP SPEED MODE

At any menu press L1, L2, R1, R2, ■, ■.

Warp Speed

SLOW MOTION MODE

At any menu press L1, L2, R1, R2, ■, ●.

NORMAL SPEED MODE

At any menu press L1, L2, R1, R2, ●, ●.

ARCTIC THUNDER

NO DRONES

At the Mode Select, press ■, ■, ●, ●, L1, R1, Start.

CATCHUP CODE

At the Mode Select, press ●, ■, ●, ●, ■, Start.

RANDOM POWER-UPS

At the Mode Select, press R1, R2, ■, ●, R1, R2, Start.

SNOWBALL POWER-UPS

At the Mode Select, press ■, ■, ■, L1, ●, Start.

Snowball Power-Ups

GRAPPLING HOOKS POWER-UPS

At the Mode Select, press ●, ●, L2, ●, ●, L1, Start.

ROOSTER POWER-UPS

At the Mode Select, press R1, R2, L2, L1, ■, Start.

SNOW BOMB POWER-UPS

At the Mode Select, press ●, ●, R1, R2, Start.

BOOST POWER-UPS

At the Mode Select, press ●, R1 (x2), ●, R2, Start.

All Invisible

ACTIVATE CLONE

At the Mode Select, press L1, L2 (x2), ●, L1, ●, Start.

ALL INVISIBLE

At the Mode Select, press ■, ●, ■, R2, ●, ●, Start.

NO POWER-UPS

At the Mode Select, press ■, ■, ●, ■, R2, ■, Start.

SUPER BOOST

At the Mode Select, press ●, L1, ■, R2, ■, L2, Start.

ARMY MEN: AIR ATTACK 2

PASSWORDS

MISSION	PASSWORD
2	Up, X, ▲, Right, Left, ■, ●, X
3	▲, ●, Down, Left, ■, ■, Up, Up
4	X, Right, Left, X, ●, ■, ■, ▲
5	Down, Down, ●, ■, ●, ■, Right, X
6	▲, X, Up, Left, Right, Left, ●, ▲
7	Left, ■, Right, Down, ●, X, X, Right
8	▲, Right, ■, ■, ●, Down, Down, X
9	Up, X, ■, Left, Right, ●, Left, Left
10	▲, Up, ●, X, ■, Down, Down, Down
11	●, ●, Up, Left, Right, X, ▲, ■
13	Left, Left, ▲, ●, X, X, Down, Right
15	Left, Right, ●, X, ■, Down, Down, ●
16	▲, ●, X, Right, Right, ●, ■, Down
18	●, X, Right, ▲, ■, Up, X, X
20	Up, X, ●, Up, Left, ■, ●, X

Passwords

ARMY MEN: SARGE'S HEROES 2

Enter the following codes as a password:

All Levels	FREEPLAY
All Weapons	GIMME

Immortal	NODIE
Invisible	NOSEEUM
Mini Mode	SHORTY
Super Sized	IMHUGE

Super Sized

Test Info	THDOTEST

Test Info

PASSWORDS

MISSION	PASSWORD
Training: Boot Camp	BOOTCAMP
Mission 1: Dinner	DINNER
Mission 2: Bridge	OVERPASS
Mission 3: Refrigerator	COOLER
Mission 4: Graveyard	NECROPOLIS
Mission 5: Castle	CITADEL
Mission 6: Tan Base	MOUSE
Mission 7: Revenge	ESCAPE
Mission 8: Desk	ESCRITOIRE
Mission 9: Bed	COT
Mission 10: Plasticville	BLUEBLUES

MISSION	PASSWORD
Mission 11: Toy Shelf	BUYME
Mission 12: Cashier	EXPRESS
Mission 13: Toy Train Town	LITTLEPEOPLE
Mission 14: Rocket Base	NUKEM
Mission 15: Pool Table	EIGHTBALL
Mission 16: Pinball Machine	BLACKKNIGHT

Pinball Machine

ATV OFFROAD FURY

TOUGHER GAME

Select Pro-career and enter the name ALLOUTAI. This should send you back to the main menu.

ALL ATVS

Select Pro-career and enter the name CHACHING. This should send you back to the main menu.

All ATVs

ALL TRACKS

Select Pro-career and enter the name WHA-TEXIT. This should send you back to the main menu.

All Tracks

BATMAN VENGEANCE

ALL CHEATS

At the main menu press L2, R2, L2, R2, ■,
■, ●, ●.

All Cheats

UNLIMITED BATCUFFS

At the main menu press ■, ●, ■, ●, L2,
R2, R2, L2.

UNLIMITED BAT LAUNCHER

At the main menu press ●, ■, ●, ■, L1,
R1, L2, R2.

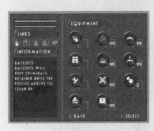

Unlimited Batcuffs

UNLIMITED ELECTRIC BATARANGS

At the main menu press L1, R1, L2, R2.

CART FURY

INFINITE CONTINUES

At the Cheats menu, L1, L2, L1, ■, ▲, ●.

UNLIMITED TIME

At the Cheats menu, ■, L1, R2, ●, ▲, R1.

INFINITE TURBO

At the Cheats menu, X, X, ■, ■, L2, L2.

LOW GRAVITY

At the Cheats menu, R2, R1, ■, ■, L1, L1.

JUMP

At the Cheats menu, L1, L2, L1, R2, **X**, **X**.

NIGHT DRIVE

At the Cheats menu, **X**, ●, ▲, L2, R2, L1.

TOGGLE FOG

At the Cheats menu, press R2, R1, **X**, ■, ■, ●.

Night Drive

Big Head

BIG HEAD

At the Cheats menu, press ▲, ■, ■, L2, L1, R2.

ROCKET WHEELS

At the Cheats menu, L1, R2, ▲, ■, ■, ▲.

ALL CARS

At the Cheats menu, press ▲, **X**, ▲, ■, L2, ▲. At the Select Driver screen press L1 to access the extra vehicles.

ALL MOVIES

At the Cheats menu, press L1, ●, R2, **X** L2, ▲. This will open all of the movies in the Danny Sullivan Theater.

All Cars

ALL TRACKS

At the Cheats menu, press R1, ▲, **X**, **X**, R2, L1.

DEATH CARS

At the Cheats menu, press L2, ■, L1, R2, R2, **X**. You will wipe out when you come in contact with another car.

DEATH WALL

At the Cheats menu, press X, ■, R2, ▲, R1, R2. This will cause you to wreck anytime you touch the wall.

PLAYER DEATH CAR

At the Cheats menu, press L1, ■, R1, R2, L2, L1. With this cheat you can take out the other cars. Caution: you will still wipe out when you accumulate enough damage.

Death Wall

MORE DRIVERS

Press R1 at the driver select.

DIFFERENT VEHICLES

Press L1 at the driver select.

CRAZY TAXI

PUSH BIKE

At the driver select hold L1 + R1, release L1 then R1. Again hold L1 + R1, release and press X.

EXPERT MODE

After you choose the time limit, hold L1 + R1 + Start. "Expert Mode" will appear in the lower corner at the driver select.

Push Bike

DISABLE ARROWS

After you choose the time limit, hold R1 + Start. "No Arrows" will appear in the lower corner at the driver select.

DISABLE DESTINATION

After you choose the time limit, hold L1 + Start. "No Destination Mark" will appear in the lower corner at the driver select.

No Arrows

ANOTHER DAY MODE

At the driver select press R1 and release, then hold R1 and press **X**. "Another Day" will appear in the lower corner.

Another Day

DAVE MIRRA FREESTYLE BMX 2

UNLOCK MOST EVERYTHING

At the Main Menu press Up, Right, Down, Left, Right, Right, Up, Down, Left, Right, Up, Left, Right, Right, Down, ■.

MIKE DIAZ

At the Main Menu press Up, Left, Down, Right, Right, Left, Up, Down, Up, Right, ■.

AMISH GUY

At the Main Menu press Up, Left, Down, Right, Right, Left, Left, Down, Up, Left, ■.

Amish Boy

All Themes

ALL BIKES

At the Main Menu press Up, Left, Down, Right, Down, Down, Right, Down, Down, Left, ■.

ALL LEVEL

At the Main Menu press Up, Down, Down, Left, Right, Down, ■.

ALL THEMES IN PARK EDITOR

At the Main Menu press Up, Left, Down, Right, Down, Up, Down, Right, Left, Left, ■.

ALL OBJECTS IN PARK EDITOR

At the Main Menu press Up, Left, Down, Right, Down, Up, Up, Down, Right, Right, ■.

ALL MOVIES

At the Main Menu press Up, Left, Down, Right, Left, Left, Right, Left, Up, Down, ■.

All Movies

MOVES

Enter the following at the Main Menu to unlock all of that character's moves:

CHARACTER	CODE
Amish Guy	Left, Right, Up, Up, Right, Down, Right, Right, ■
Colin Mackay	Left, Right, Right, Up, Left, Right, Right, Up, ■
Dave Mirra	Left, Right, Up, Up, Left, Right, Up, Up, ■
Joey Garcia	Left, Right, Up, Right, Down, Up, Down, Right, ■
John Englebert	Left, Right, Left, Left, Down, Up, Left, Left, ■
Kenan Harkin	Left, Right, Left, Down, Up, Down, Down, Down, ■
Leigh Ramsdell	Left, Right, Down, Left, Left, Right, Down, Left, ■
Mike Laird	Left, Right, Right, Right, Left, Right, Up, Right, ■
Rick Moliterno	Left, Right, Up, Up, Up, Down, Left, Up, ■
Ryan Nyquist	Left, Right, Down, Down, Down, Up, Up, Down, ■
Scott Wirch	Left, Right, Right, Right, Up, Down, Left, Right, ■
Slim Jim	Left, Right, Down, Left, Up, Left, Right, Left, ■
Tim Mirra	Left, Right, Right, Up, Down, Up, Down, Up, ■
Todd Lyons	Left, Right, Down, Down, Left, Right, Left, Down, ■
Troy McMurray	Left, Right, Left, Left, Up, Down, Up, Left, ■
Zach Shaw	Left, Right, Left, Down, Left, Up, Right, Down, ■

BIKES

Enter the following at the Main Menu to unlock all of that character's bikes:

CHARACTER	CODE
Colin Mackay	Down, Down, Right (x5), Up, ■
Dave Mirra	Down, Down, Up, Right, Up, Right, Up, Up, ■

Dave Mirra

Joey Garcia	Down, Down, Up, Right, Left, Left, Down, Right, ■
John Englebert	Down, Down, Left, Up, Left, Up, Left, Left, ■
Kenan Harkin	Down, Down, Left, Up, Down, Right, Down, Down, ■
Leigh Ramsdell	Down, Down, Down, Up, Left, Left, Down, Left, ■
Mike Laird	Down, Down, Right, Left, Down, Up, Up, Right, ■
Rick Moliterno	Down, Down, Up, Left, Right, Right, Left, Up, ■
Ryan Nyquist	Down (x5), Right, Up, Down, ■
Scott Wirch	Down, Down, Right, Up, Down, Down, Left, Right, ■
Tim Mirra	Down, Down, Right, Left, Down, Right, Down, Up, ■
Todd Lyons	Down (x4), Left, Right, Left, Down, ■
Troy McMurray	Down, Down, Left, Down, Right, Left, Up, Left, ■
Zach Shaw	Down, Down, Left, Down, Up, Right, Right, Down, ■

LEVELS

Enter the following at the Main Menu to unlock all of that character's levels:

CHARACTER	CODE
Colin Mackay	Up, Up, Right, Left, Up, Right, Right, Up, ■
Dave Mirra	Up, Up, Up, Right, Up, Left, Up, Up, ■
Joey Garcia	Up (x4), Down, Down, Down, Right, ■
John Englebert	Up, Up, Left, Down, Right, Down, Left, Left, ■
Kenan Harkin	Up, Up, Left, Left, Down, Up, Down, Down, ■
Leigh Ramsdell	Up, Up, Down, Up, Left, Down, Down, Left, ■
Mike Laird	Up, Up, Right, Down, Down, Right, Up, Right, ■
Rick Moliterno	Up, Up, Up, Down, Right, Right, Left, Up, ■
Ryan Nyquist	Up, Up, Down, Down, Left, Right, Up, Down, ■
Scott Wirch	Up, Up, Right, Up, Left, Left, Left, Right, ■
Tim Mirra	Up, Up, Right, Down, Right, Left, Down, Up, ■

Tim Mirra

Todd Lyons	Up, Up, Down, Up, Right, Right, Left, Down, ■
Troy McMurray	Up, Up, Left, Up, Up, Right, Up, Left, ■
Zach Shaw	Up, Up, Left, Right, Down, Down, Right, Down, ■

MOVIES

Enter the following at the Main Menu to unlock all of that character's movies:

CHARACTER	CODE
Colin Mackey	Left, Left, Right, Right, Down, Down, Right, Up, ■
Dave Mirra	Left, Left, Up, Right, Up, Left, Up, Up, ■
Joey Garcia	Left, Left, Up, Up, Down, Right, Down, ■
Kenan Harkin	Left (x4), Right, Right, Down, Down, ■

Continued

CHARACTER	CODE
Leigh Ramsdell	Left, Left, Down, Down, Left, Right, Down, Left, ■
Luc-E	Left, Left, Right, Right, Down, Down, Right, Up, ■

Luc-E

Mike Laird	Left, Left, Right, Up, Up, Right, Up, Right, ■
Rick Moliterno	Left, Left, Up, Down, Right, Left, Left, Up, ■
Ryan Nyquist	Left, Left, Down, Right, Down, Right, Up, Down, ■
Scott Wirch	Left, Left, Right, Up, Up, Up, Left, Right, ■
Tim Mirra	Left, Left, Right, Up, Down, Left, Down, Up, ■
Todd Lyons	Left, Left, Down, Up, Up, Right, Left, Down, ■
Troy McMurray	Left, Left, Left, Down, Up, Right, Up, Left, ■
Zach Shaw	Left, Left, Left, Right, Left, Down, Right, Down, ■

COMPETITION OUTFIT

Enter the following at the Main Menu to unlock all of that character's competition outfits:

OUTFIT	CODE
Colin Mackey	Up, Down, Right, Down, Up, Right, Right, Up, ■

Colin Mackey

OUTFIT	CODE
Dave Mirra	Up, Down, Up, Down, Right, Left, Up, Up, ■
Joey Garcia	Up, Down, Up, Left, Down, Right, Down, Right, ■
Kenan Harkin	Up, Down, Left, Down, Left, Up, Down, Up, ■
Leigh Ramsdell	Up, Down, Down, Left, Down, Down, Down, Left, ■
Luc-E	Up, Down, Left, Down, Left, Right, Left, Left, ■
Mike Laird	Up, Up, Down, Down, Left, Right, Right, Left, ■
Rick Moliterno	Up, Down, Up (x4), Left, Up, ■
Ryan Nyquist	Up, Down, Down, Left, Down, Up, Up, Down, ■
Scott Wirch	Up, Down, Right, Down, Up, Right, Right, Up, ■
Tim Mirra	Up, Down, Right, Left, Left, Up, Down, Up, ■
Todd Lyons	Up, Down, Down, Right, Up, Left, Left, Down, ■
Troy McMurray	Up, Down, Left, Down, Right, Left, Up, Left, ■
Zach Shaw	Up, Down, Left, Right, Down, Down, Right, Down, ■

GAUNTLET: DARK LEGACY

CHEAT CODES

Enter the following as your name. You can only use one at a time.

EFFECT	CODE
10,000 Gold	10000K
9 Potions And Keys	ALLFUL
Pojo the Chicken	EGG911

Pojo the Chicken

EFFECT	CODE
Small Enemies	DELTA1
Invincible	INVULN
Invisible	000000
Anti Death	1ANGEL
Full Turbo Meter	PURPLE
Faster	XSPEED
X-Ray	PEEKIN
Reflective Shots	REFLEX
3-Way Shot	MENAGE
Supershot	SSHOTS
Rapid Fire	QCKSHT

SECRET COSTUMES

Enter the following as your name. Each code is a different costume.

Secret Costumes

CLASS	COSTUME CODES
Dwarf	ICE600
	NUD069
Jester	KJH105
	PNK666
	STX222
Knight	ARV984
	BAT900
	CSS222
	DARTHC
	DIB626
	KAO292
	RIZ721

CLASS	COSTUME CODES
Knight cont.	SJB964
	STG333
	TAK118
Valkyrie	AYA555
	CEL721
	TWN300
Warrior	CAS400
	MTN200
	RAT333
Wizard	DES700
	GARM00
	GARM99
	SKY100
	SUM224

GRAND THEFT AUTO III

TANK

Press ● (x6), R1, L2, L1, ▲, ●, ▲ during game play. Repeat as many times as needed.

Tank

LOWER WANTED LEVEL

Press R2 (x2), L1, R2, Up, Down, Up, Down, Up, Down during game play.

HIGHER WANTED LEVEL

Press R2 (x2), L1, R2, Left, Right, Left, Right, Left during game play.

ALL WEAPONS

Press R2 (x2), L1, R2, Left, Down, Right, Up, Left, Down, Right, Up during game play.

FULL HEALTH

Press R2 (x2), L1, R1, Left, Down, Right, Up, Left, Down, Right, Up during game play.

FULL ARMOR

Press R2 (x2), L1, L2, Left, Down, Right, Up, Left, Down, Right, Up during game play.

MONEY

Press R2 (x2), L1, L1, Left, Down, Right, Up, Left, Down, Right, Up during game play.

DESTROY ALL CARS

Press L2, R2, L1, R1, L2, R2, ▲, ■, ●, ▲, L2, L1

Destroy all Cars

IMPROVED DRIVING

Press R1, L1, R2, L1, Left, R1 (x2), ▲ during game play. Press L3 to hop.

FOG

Press L1, L2, R1, R2 (x2), R1, L2, X during game play.

OVERCAST

Press L1, L2, R1, R2 (x2), R1, L2, ■ during game play.

RAIN

Press L1, L2, R1, R2 (x2), R1, L2, ●
during game play.

CLEAR SKIES

Press L1, L2, R1, R2 (x2), R1, L2, ▲
during game play.

Rain

SPEED UP TIME

Press ● (x3), ■ (x5), L1, ▲, ●, ▲ during game play.

CHANGE OUTFIT

Press Right, Down, Left, Up, L1, L2, Up, Left, Down, Right during game play.
Enter again for another outfit.

Change Outfit

PEDESTRIANS RIOT

Press Down, Up, Left, Up, X, R1, R2, L2, L1 during game play.

PEDESTRIANS ATTACK

Press Down, Up, Left, Up, X, R1, R2, L1, L2 during game play.

PEDESTRIANS CRAZY

Press R2, R1, ▲, X, L2, L1, Up, Down during game play.

PEDESTRIANS FIGHTING

Press Right, R2, ●, R1, L2, Down, L1, R1 during game play.

HALF-LIFE

The following codes will appear to the right if entered correctly.

Cheat Codes

SLOW MOTION

Go to the cheat screen and press Right, ■, Up, ▲, Right, ■, Up, ▲.

INFINITE AMMO

Go to the cheat screen and press Down, X, Left, ●, Down, X, Left, ●.

XEN GRAVITY

Go to the cheat screen and press Up, ▲, Down, X, Up, ▲, Down, X.

INVINCIBILITY

Go to the cheat screen and press Left, ■, Up, ▲, Right, ●, Down, X.

INVISIBILITY

Go to the cheat screen and press Left, ■, Right, ●, Left, ■, Right, ●.

ALIEN MODE

Go to the cheat screen and press Up, ▲, Up, ▲, Up, ▲, Up, ▲.

KINETICA

TURBO START

When Go appears, press Up + Gas.

Turbo Start

LEGACY OF KAIN: SOUL REAVER 2

ALL BONUS MATERIALS

At the main menu press Left, ▲, Right, ▲, Down, ●, X.

Bonus Materials

LEGO RACERS 2

MARTIAN

At the main menu press Right, Left, Right, Up, Down, Left, Right, Up, Up.

MARS TRACKS

Pause the game and press Left, Left, Right, Right, Left, Left, Right, Right, Down, Left, Right.

WIDE ANGLE

Pause the game and press Left, Left, Left, Right, Right, Right, Up, Up, Up, Down, Down, Down, Left, Left, Left, Right, Right, Right.

LE MANS 24 HOURS

ALL CARS

Select Championship and enter your name as ACO.

ALL TRACKS

Select Championship and enter your name as SPEEDY.

ALL CHAMPIONSHIPS

Select Championship and enter your name as NUMBAT.

LE MANS

Select Championship and enter your name as WOMBAT.

CREDITS

Select Championship and enter your name as HEINEY.

NASCAR HEAT 2002

HORNBALL

In Single Race or Head-to-Head, enter the following cheats at the Race Day screen. Press Up to fire.

EFFECT	CHEAT
Hornball in race	Up, Down, Left, Right, R1, Up, Up
Hornball in practice	Up, Down, Left, Right, R1, Down, Down

NBA STREET

CHEATS

After selecting your players you will have an opportunity to enter codes. Use the
■, ▲, ●, X buttons to enter the following. The first number corresponds to the
number of times you press ■, the second is for ▲, the third for ● and the last
for X. After you enter these press any direction to enter the code. These numbers match up to icons on screen as follows

NUMBER	ICON
0	Basketball
1	Record Player
2	Shoe
3	Backboard
4	Bullhorn

For example, the code for Big Heads is 4 1 2 1 or Bullhorn, Record Player, Shoe,
Record Player. Here you would press ■ four times, ▲ once, ● two times and X
one time. Then, press in any direction to activate the code. It will tell you if you
have entered a code correctly.

Cheats

EFFECT	CODE
No Cheats	1 1 1 1
ABA Ball	0 1 1 0
WNBA Ball	0 1 2 0
NuFX Ball	0 1 3 0
EA Big Ball	0 1 4 0
Beach Ball	0 1 1 2

Continued

EFFECT	CODE
Medicine Ball	0 1 1 3
Volleyball	0 1 1 4
Soccer Ball	0 2 1 0
Big Heads	4 1 2 1
Tiny Heads	4 2 0 2
Tiny Players	4 0 4 0
Casual Uniforms	1 1 0 0
Authentic Uniforms	0 0 1 1
ABA Socks	4 4 4 4
Athletic Joe "The Show"	1 2 0 1
Springtime Joe "The Show"	1 1 0 1
Summertime Joe "The Show"	1 0 0 1
Player Names	0 1 2 3
No HUD Display	1 4 1 2
No Player Indicators	4 0 0 4
No Shot Indicator	4 3 2 4
No Shot Clock	4 4 0 3
Unlimited Turbo	2 0 3 0
No Juice	1 4 4 3
Easy Distance Shots	2 1 3 0
Harder Distance Shots	2 2 3 0
Captain Quicks	3 0 2 1
Mad Handles	3 2 1 0
Mega Dunking	3 0 1 0
Sticky Fingers	3 4 1 0
Super Swats	3 3 1 0
Ultimate Power	3 1 1 0
Less Blocks	3 1 2 3
Less Steals	3 1 4 0
No 2-Pointers	3 3 0 3
No Alley-Oops	3 4 1 2
No Dunks	3 0 1 2
Less Gamebreakers	1 3 4 2
More Gamebreakers	1 4 3 2

EFFECT	CODE
No Gamebreakers	1 4 4 2
No Auto Replays	1 2 1 1
Explosive Rims	1 2 4 0

NHL 2001

PLAY AS "THE HAMMER"

Enter the Rosters menu and select Create Player. Use the name "Hammer" for the player's first name and you will be referred to as "The Hammer" during gameplay.

PLAY AS "ANIMAL"

Enter the Rosters menu and select Create Player. Use the name "Animal" for the player's first name and you will be referred to as "Animal" during gameplay.

NHL HITZ 20-02

CHEATS

After selecting your players, you will have a chance to enter codes by changing three icons with the ■, ▲ and ●. Use the ■ to change the first icon, the ▲ for second and the ● for the third. You will then need to press in the direction indicated. For example, to enter the code for 1st to 7 Wins, you would press ■ three times, ▲ two times and ● three times. Then press Left on the Directional pad.

EFFECT	CHEAT
Input More Codes	3 3 3 Right
Ignore Last Code	0 1 0 Down
1st to 7 Wins	3 2 3 Left
Win Fights For Goals	2 0 2 Left
No Crowd	2 1 0 Right
Show Hot Spot	2 0 1 Up
Show Shot Speed	1 0 1 Up
Rain	1 4 1 Left
Snow	1 2 1 Left

Continued

EFFECT	CHEAT
Big Puck	1 2 1 Up
Huge Puck	3 2 1 Up
Bulldozer Puck	2 1 2 Left
Hockey Ball	1 3 3 Left
Tennis Ball	1 3 2 Down
No Puck Out of Play	1 1 1 Down
Big Head Player	2 0 0 Right
Huge Head Player	3 0 0 Right
Big Head Team	2 2 0 Left
Huge Head Team	3 3 0 Left
Always Big Hits	2 3 4 Down
Late Hits	3 2 1 Down
Pinball Boards	4 2 3 Right
Domino Effect	0 1 2 Right
Turbo Boost	0 0 2 Up
Infinite Turbo	4 1 3 Right
No Fake Shots	4 2 4 Down
No One-Timers	2 1 3 Left
Skills Versus	2 2 2 Down
Hitz Time	1 0 4 Right

QUAKE III: REVOLUTION

LEVEL SKIP

During a game, hold L1 + R1 + R2 + Select and press X, ●, ■, ▲, X, ●, ■, ▲. You will automatically win the match.

Level Skip

RAYMAN 2: REVOLUTION

MINI-GAMES

Select Options. Then choose Language. Select Voices and highlight Raymanian. Do not select it, just highlight it. Now, press and hold:

L1 + R1

And enter:

L2, R2, L2, R2, L2, R2.

If you performed the code correctly, you'll be taken immediately to a new menu where you can choose between three new mini-games.

NAMES IN BABY SOCCER

You will have to first enable the "Extra Bonus Mini-Games" cheat and select Baby Soccer. While you play this game you can press and hold:

L1 + R1

And Enter:

L2, R2, L2, R2, L2, R2.

Once you have entered the code, the Globox who are playing soccer will have their names displayed above their heads while you play.

CHEAT MENU

During Gameplay you can pause your game and then select Sound. Now highlight the Mute selection. Do not select it, just highlight it. Now, Press and hold:

L1 + R1

And enter:

L2, R2, L2, R2, L2, R2.

If you did it right, you'll see a new menu pop up with cheat options. You can turn them on or off by highlight them an hitting the **X** button. If the cheat is red, it is turned on. If it is blue, it is turned off.

RUMBLE RACING

CUP PASSWORDS

In the Game Options select Password and enter the following. Once you open the Pro Cup 1, you get the Pro Class vehicles, and the same with Elite.

PASSWORD	NEW CUP	NEW VEHICLE	NEW TRACK
KOZIEC1PU	Rookie Cup 2	Dragon	So Refined
KZOIEC2PI	EA Rookie Cup	Mandrake	Passing Through
OORKIEPUC	Pro Cup 1	Maelstrom	Sun Burn
P1PROC1PU	Pro Cup 2	Cataclysm	Falls Down
Q2PROC2YT	Pro Cup 3	Escargot	The Gauntlet
P3PROC3LM	EA Pro Cup	El Diablo	Touch and Go

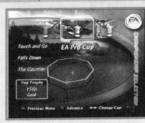

Touch and Go

AEPPROPUC	Elite Cup 1	Road Kill	Surf and Turf
ILETEC1MB	Elite Cup 2	Jolly Roger	Coal Cuts
ILCTEC2VB	Elite Cup 3	Malice	Wild Kingdom
ILQTEC3PU	Elite Cup 4	Direwolf	Over Easy
LEAITEPUC	EA Elite Cup	Blue Devil	Outer Limits
YEAMPLOWW	EA Stunt Cup	None	None
ZEAGTLUKE	None	None	Circus Minimus

Circus Minimus

VEHICLE PASSWORDS

VEHICLE	PASSWORD
Cobalt	TLACOBTLA
Revolution	PTOATRTOI

Revolution

High Roller	HGIROLREL
Stinger	AMHBRAAMH
Buckshot	UBTCKSTOH
Sporticus	OPSRTISUC
Gamecus	BSUIGASUM

Gamecus

Van Itty	VTYANIYTT
Redneck Roctet	KCEROCTEK
Thor	THTORHROT

Continued

VEHICLE	PASSWORD
Road Trip	ABOGOBOGA
Interceptor	CDAAPTNIA

Interceptor

XXS TOMCAT	NALDSHHSD
Vortex	1AREXT1AR

Vortex

SHAUN PALMER'S PRO SNOWBOARDER

Highlight Options at the Main Menu and enter the following:

UNLOCK	CHEAT
All Cheats	Hold Right + L2 and press ▲, ▲, ●, ▲

All Cheats

Max All Stats	Hold Right + L1 and press ▲, ▲, ●, ▲

Max All Stats

All Boards	Hold Left + L2 and press ▲, ▲, ●, ▲

All Boards

UNLOCK	CHEAT
Secret Boarders	Hold Left + L1 and press ▲, ▲, ●, ▲

Secret Boarders

All Movies	Hold Left + R1 and press ▲, ▲, ●, ▲

All Movies

All Levels	Hold Right + R1 and press ▲, ▲, ●, ▲

All Levels

SMUGGLER'S RUN 2: HOSTILE TERRITORY

INVISIBILITY

Pause the game and press R1, L1, L1, R2, L1, L1, L2.

LIGHT CARS

Pause the game and press L1, R1, R1, L2, R2, R2.

NO GRAVITY

Pause the game and press R1, R2, R1, R2, Up, Up, Up.

Invisibility

SLOWER SPEED

Pause the game and press R2, L2, L1, R1, Left, Left, Left. You can enter this code up to three times from the normal speed.

FASTER SPEED

Pause the game and press R1, L1, L2, R2, Right, Right, Right. You can enter this code up to three times from the normal speed.

STAR WARS: STARFIGHTER

Enter the following codes at the Codes screen in the Options Menu:

ARTIST'S STORYBOARD

JAMEZ

You will be taken back to the Code screen when the slideshow is finished.

Christmas Cinema

CHRISTMAS CINEMA

WOZ

Nym will find a Disco Santa

JAR JAR MODE

JARJAR

All of the controls will be reversed. Disable this by returning to the Option Menu and choosing the default game options.

SIMON DAY

SIMON

A picture of the LEC team will be shown singling out a certain Simon.

UNLOCK EXPERIMENTAL N-1 FIGHTER

BLUENSF

Simon Day

Another ship will be added to the list of ships in the Bonus Missions. However, you will not be able to select the ship unless you achieve a Gold rating on every mission after defeating the game, or enter the OVERSEER code.

INVINCIBLE MODE

MINIME

UNLOCK EVERYTHING (ALMOST)

OVERSEER

This will not open multi-player levels.

UNLOCK MULTI-PLAYER MODES
ANDREW

DIRECTOR MODE
DIRECTOR

This will randomly change the camera angles during gameplay. However, the control will be lost. You will be able to press R1 to zoom in occasionally and you can use the Select button to change the camera.

Disable this by returning to the Options Menu and restoring the Default settings.

PROGRAMMER'S HIDDEN MESSAGE
LTDJGD

NO H.U.D. (HEADS UP DISPLAY)
NOHUD

"Bonus Feature Unlocked" will pop up on the Codes screen to confirm that you have entered the code correctly.

CHARACTER SKETCHES
HEROES

Character Sketches

VIEW THE CREDITS
CREDITS

VIEW THE GALLERY
SHIPS

VIEW PLANET SKETCHES AND MORE
PLANETS

DEFAULT

Default

DEFAULT MESSAGE
SHOTS or SIZZLE

Burger Droid

BURGER DROID

Enter the DIRECTOR code. Select Fighter Training in the bonus missions and a special Droid Chef will be able to be seen on an asteroid.

DEVELOPMENT TEAM PIC

TEAM

STAR WARS: SUPER BOMBAD RACING

BOBA FETT

At the main menu press ■, ●, ▲, ●, ■.

TANK

At the main menu press ●, ■, ●, ■ or ●, ▲, ■, ●, ▲, ■.

EVERYBODY IS A KAADU

At the main menu press L1, R1, L2, R2.

Boba Fett

Shaak Races

LET THE SHAAK RACES BEGIN!

At the main menu press Up, Right, Down, Left, Select.

GRRL POWER ENABLED!

At the main menu press Down, Select, Up, Select, Left, Right, Select.

SPACE FREIGHTER ARENA

At the main menu press L1, R1, Select, ●.

Girl Power

Arena Mode

SUPER ARENA MODE

At the main menu press Up, Up, Down, Down, Left, Right, Left.

BACKWARDS FACING MODE

At the main menu press L2 (x4), ●, Select.

INFINITE BOOST MODE

At the main menu press L1, R2, L1, R2, ■, Select.

SUPER SPINNING MODE

At the main menu press Up, Left, Down, Right, Left, Up, Down.

Infinite Boost Mode

Slip 'n Slide

SLIP 'N SLIDE MODE

At the main menu press Left, Right, ■, ●, L1, L2.

ALL DEATH STAR MODE

At the main menu press R1 (x4), Up, Left.
All weapons are Death Stars

SUPER HONK MODE

At the main menu press ● (x4), L2, Select.

SUPER SPEEDY MODE

At the main menu press L1 (x4), R2, ■.

JAWA LANGUAGE

At the main menu press Select, Select, Select, ■. This will change every word to Utinni.

Jawa Language

Battle Droid Language

BATTLE DROID LANGUAGE

At the main menu press Select, Select, Select, Up. This will change every word to Roger.

ENGLISH LANGUAGE

At the main menu press Select, Select, Select, ●.

FRENCH LANGUAGE

At the main menu press Select, Select, Select, R2.

GERMAN LANGUAGE

At the main menu press Select, Select, Select, L1.

ITALIAN LANGUAGE

At the main menu press Select, Select, Select, L2.

SPANISH LANGUAGE

At the main menu press Select, Select, Select, R1.

SUNNY GARCIA SURFING

ALL SURFBOARDS

At the title screen, hold R1 + L1 and press Left, ●, Up, Down, ●, Left, Down, ●, X.

ALL SURFERS

At the title screen, hold R1 + L1 and press Left, ●, Up, Right, ●, Left, Left.

THE SIMPSONS: ROAD RAGE

HIDDEN CHARACTERS

Set the system date to the following to open the secret characters:

DATE	CHARACTER
Jan 1	Happy New Year Krusty the Klown

Krusty the Klown

Oct 31	Happy Halloween Bart

Bart

Continued

DATE	CHARACTER
Nov 22, 2001	Happy Thanksgiving Marge
Nov 28, 2002	Happy Thanksgiving Marge

Marge

Dec 25	Merry Christmas Apu

Apu

TONY HAWK'S PRO SKATER 3

ALL CHEATS

Select Cheats from the Options menu and type in "backdoor." Access the cheats from the pause menu.

All Cheats

ALL MOVIES

Select Cheats from the Options menu and type in "Peepshow."

All Movies

TWISTED METAL: BLACK

Set the control option to Classic for the following codes.

WEAPONS INTO HEALTH

During a game, hold L1 + R1 + L2 + R2 and press ▲, X, ■, ●.

GOD MODE

During a game, hold L1 + R1 + L2 + R2 and press Up, X, Left, ●.

INVULNERABILITY

During a game, hold L1 + R1 + L2 + R2 and press Right, Left, Down, Up.

MEGA GUNS

During a game, hold L1 + R1 + L2 + R2 and press X, X, ▲.

Mega Guns

KILLER WEAPONS
ONE HIT KILLS

During a game, hold L1 + R1 + L2 + R2 and press X, X, Up. Re-enter the code to disable it.

Killer Weapon

UNREAL TOURNAMENT

4 PLAYER WITH ILINK

You can play up to 4 player multiplayer with 4 PlayStation 2 systems and a 4 point fire wire hub. Connect fire wire from each PS 2 to the hub.

Start a multiplayer game, pause the game and press Left, ●, Left, Right, ■, Right. It should say "Waiting For Other Players." Have each person hit Start to join the game.

WILD WILD RACING

SECRET MENU

At the options menu hold ■ and press Up, ●, Down, ●, Left, Right, Left, Right, ●.

TOP SECRET MENU

Enter your name as NORTHEND. This will open a Top Secret Menu in the Secret Menu.

Secret Menu

Top Secret Menu

WORLD DESTRUCTION LEAGUE: WAR JETZ

PASSWORDS

ARENA	PASSWORD
Panama 2	JBVKWNBBCBQM
Panama 3	MDKKWYFTKBQM
Australia 1	MHZKWTJMQBQM
Australia 2	ZBCKXPBHNBQM
Australia 3	LDRKXYFZTBQM
Thailand 1	ZHHKXJJTBBQM
Thailand 2	TBPKYZBVHBQM
Thailand 3	KFFPJRFNPBQN
Rhine River 1	YJVPJCJGVBQN
Rhine River 2	FCNPKXBVWBQN
Rhine River 3	PGDPKGFPDBQN
New York City 1	KKSPKRJHKBQN
New York City 2	VBFKPLHBWZBQN
New York City 3	WJYPLWFQGBQN
Antarctica 1	CMPPLHJJNBQN
Antarctica 2	RKFPMYBZHBQN
Antarctica 3	GNVPMQFSNBQN
San Francisco 1	TRLPMBJLVBQN
San Francisco 2	SVMPNFBFVBQN
San Francisco 3	RXDPNHFYDBQN
Valhalla 1	XBXPNGKRKBQN
Valhalla 2	LPXKVMCQZBQM
Valhalla 3	QSMKVSGKHBQM

SUPER CHEATS

Enter SPRLZY as a code.

ALL CHEATS

Enter TWLVCHTS as a code.

Super Cheats

All Cheats

LEVEL SELECT

Enter JMPTT as a code.

Level Select

RAPID FIRE

Enter FRHS as a code.

SPEED SHOTS

Enter NSTNT as a code.

DUAL FIRE

Enter NDBMBS as a code.

SPIN SHOTS

Enter DZZY as a code.

SHIELDS ON ROLL

Enter SCRW as a code.

INVULNERABLE

Enter DNGDM as a code.

FAST PLANES

Enter ZPPY as a code.

BIGGER GUNS

Enter HMMR as a code.

BIGGEST GUNS

Enter QD as a code.

THICK ARMOR

Enter MRRMR as a code.

TOP GUN MODE
Enter DH as a code.

DOUBLE BUX
Enter TWFSTD as a code.

EXTRA 10 BUX
Enter WNNNGS as a code.

WEAPON UP AT 3
Enter PYRS as a code.

OVERLORDS
Enter VRLRDS as a code.

VALHALLA
Enter WNRLFST as a code.

GHOST MODE
Enter SNKY as a code.

SWITCH PLANE
Enter NDCSN as a code.

PLANE WINS
Enter SMSHNG as a code.

SHOW BOXES
Enter BXDRW as a code.

WAYPOINTS
Enter WYPNT as a code.

EVERY MOVIE
Enter GRTD as a code.

Every Movie

ZONE OF THE ENDERS

UNLOCK VERSUS MODE
●, X, Right, Left, Right, Left, Down, Down, Up, Up.

This will open Versus mode with all of the available characters and environments.

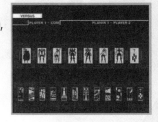

Unlock Versus Mode

THE GAMES

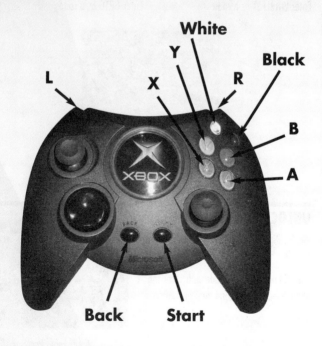

AMPED: FREESTYLE SNOWBOARDING

RAVEN

Enter RidinwRaven at the Cheat Menu.

ARCTIC THUNDER

NO DRONES

At the Mode Select, press X, X, Y, Y, White, Black, Start.

CATCH UP CODE

At the Mode Select, press Y, X, Y, Y, X, Start.

RANDOM POWER-UPS

At the Mode Select, press Black, R, X, Y, Black, R, Start.

SNOWBALL POWER-UPS

At the Mode Select, press X, X, X, White, Y, Start.

GRAPPLING HOOKS POWER-UPS

At the Mode Select, press Y, Y, L, Y, Y, White, Start.

ROOSTER POWER-UPS

At the Mode Select, press Black, R, L, White, X, Start.

SNOW BOMB POWER-UPS

At the Mode Select, press Y, Y, Black, R, Start.

BOOST POWER-UPS

At the Mode Select, press Y, Black, Black, Y, R, Start.

ACTIVATE CLONE

At the Mode Select, press White, L, L, Y, White, Y, Start.

ALL INVISIBLE

At the Mode Select, press X, Y, X, R, Y, Y, Start.

NO POWER-UPS

At the Mode Select, press X, X, Y, X, R, X, Start.

SUPER BOOST

At the Mode Select, press Y, White, X, R, X, L, Start.

CEL DAMAGE

ALL CARS, COURSES AND MODES

Enter ENCHILADA! as your name.

All Cars, Courses and Modes

DAVE MIRRA FREESTYLE BMX 2

ALL BIKES

CHARACTER	CODE
Dave Mirra	Down, Down, Up, Right, Up, Right, Up, Up, X button
Ryan Nyquist	Down, Down, Down, Down, Down, Right, Up, Down, X button
Troy McMurray	Down, Down, Left, Down, Right, Left, Up, Left, X button
Mike Laird	Down, Down, Right, Left, Down, Up, Up, Right, X button

CHARACTER	CODE
Tim Mirra	Down, Down, Right, Left, Down, Right, Down, Up, X button
Kenan Harkin	Down, Down, Left, Up, Down, Right, Down, Down, X button
Leigh Ramsdell	Down, Down, Down, Up, Left, Left, Down, Left, X button
Joey Garcia	Down, Down, Up, Right, Left, Left, Down, Right, X button
Rick Moliterno	Down, Down, Up, Left, Right, Right, Left, Up, X button
Todd Lyons	Down, Down, Down, Down, Left, Right, Left, Down, X button
John Englebert	Down, Down, Left, Up, Left, Up, Left, Left, X button
Scott Wirch	Down, Down, Right, Up, Down, Down, Left, Right, X button
Colin Mackay	Down, Down, Right, Right, Right, Right, Right Up, X button
Zach Shaw	Down, Down, Left, Down, Up, Right, Right, Down, X button

ALL LEVELS

CHARACTER	CODE
Dave Mirra	Up, Up, Up Right, Up Left, Up, Up, X button
Ryan Nyquist	Up, Up, Down, Down, Left, Right, Up, Down, X button
Troy McMurray	Up, Up, Left, Up, Up, Right, Up, Left, X button
Mike Laird	Up, Up, Right, Down, Down, Right, Up, Right, X button
Tim Mirra	Up, Up, Right, Down, Right, Left, Down, Up, X button
Kenan Harkin	Up, Up, Left, Left, Down, Up, Down, Down, X button
Leigh Ramsdell	Up, Up, Down, Up, Left, Down, Down Left, X button
Joey Garcia	Up, Up, Up, Up, Down, Down, Right, X button
Rick Moliterno	Up, Up, Up, Down, Right, Right, Left, Up, Sqaure
Todd Lyons	Up, Up, Down Up, Right, Right, Left, Down, X button
John Englebert	Up, Up, Left, Down, Right, Down, Left, Left, Sqaure
Scott Wirch	Up, Up, Right, Up, Left, Left, Left, Right, X button
Colin Mackay	Up, Up, Right, Left, Up, Right, Right, Up, X button
Zach Shaw	Up, Up, Left, Right, Down, Down, Right, Down, X button

ALL SIGNATURE TRICKS

CHARACTER	CODE
Dave Mirra	Left, Right, Up, Up, Left, Right, Up, Up, X button
Ryan Nyquist	Left, Right, Down, Down, Down, Up, Up, Down, X button
Troy McMurray	Left, Right, Left, Left, Up, Down, Up, Left, X button
Mike Laird	Left, Right, Right, Right, Left, Right, Up, Right, X button

Continued

CHARACTER	CODE
Tim Mirra	Left, Right, Right, Up, Down, Up, Down, Up, X button
Kenan Harkin	Left, Right, Left, Down, Up, Down, Down, Down X button
Leigh Ramsdell	Left, Right, Down, Left, Left, Right, Down, Left, X button
Joey Garcia	Left, Right, Up, Right, Down, Up, Down, Right, X button
Rick Moliterno	Left, Right, Up, Up, Up, Down, Left, Up, X button
Todd Lyons	Left, Right, Down, Down, Left, Right, Left, Down, X button
John Englebert	Left, Right, Left, Left, Down, Up, Left, Left, X button
Scott Wirch	Left, Right, Right, Right, Up, Down, Left, Right, X button
Colin Mackay	Left, Right, Right, Up, Left, Right, Right, Up, X button
Zach Shaw	Left, Right, Left, Down, Left, Up, Right, Down, X button
Slim Jim Guy	Left, Right, Down, Left, Up, Left, Right, Left, X button
Amish Air	Left, Right, Up, Up, Right, Down, Right, Right, X button

RIDER COMPETITION OUTFITS

CHARACTER	CODE
Dave Mirra	Right, Right, Up, Right, Down, Down, Left, Left, X button
Ryan Nyquist	Right, Right, Down, Down, Left, Up, Up, Down, X button
Troy McMurray	Right, Right, Left, Up, Left, Left, Up, Left, X button
Mike Laird	Right, Right, Right, Up, Down, Down, Up, Right, X button
Tim Mirra	Right, Right, Right, Down, Down, Right, Down, Up, X button
Kenan Harkin	Right, Right, Left, Down, Up, Left, Down, Down, X button
Leigh Ramsdell	Right, Right, Down, Left, Up, Down, Down, Left, X button
Joey Garcia	Right, Right, Up, Down, Up, Right, Down, Right, X button
Rick Moliterno	Right, Right, Up, Up, Up, Right, Left, Up, X button
Todd Lyons	Right, Right, Down, Left, Left, Up, Left, Down, X button
John Englebert	Right, Right, Left, Right, Up, Up, Left, Left, X button
Scott Wirch	Right, Right, Right, Up, Left, Left, Left, Right, X button
Colin Mackay	Right, Right, Right, Left, Right, Up, Right, Up, X button
Zach Shaw	Right, Right, Left, Left, Down, Down, Right, Down, X button

DEAD OR ALIVE 3

EIN AND RANDOM SELECT

Finish Story Mode with all 16 characters. Use Hayate in Survival Mode or Time Attack Mode. Enter EIN as your name.

Random Select

FUZION FRENZY

FIRST PERSON MODE

Pause the game, hold L and press Y, B, Y, B. Repeat to disable.

MUTANT MODE

Pause the game, hold L and press Y, B, X, X. Repeat the code for Mutant Mode 2, again for Mutant Mode 3 and a fourth time to disable Mutant Mode.

First Person Mode

WELSH

Pause the game, hold L and press Y, Y, Y, Y. Repeat to disable.

SQUEAKY VOICES

Pause the game, hold L and press Y, X, Y, Y. Repeat to disable.

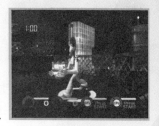

Mutant Mode

NASCAR THUNDER 2002

EXTRA DRIVERS

At the driver creation screen enter the following names:

NAME
Audrey Clark
Benny Parsons
Buster Auton
Cheryl King
Chuck Spicer
Crissy Hillsworth
Daryl Wolfe
Dave Alpern
Dave Nichols
Diane Grubb
Dick Paysor
Jim Hannigan
Joey Joulwan
Josh Neelon
Katrina Goode
Ken Patterson
Kristi Jones
Mandy Misiak
Michelle Emser
Rick Edwards
Rick Humphrey
Sasha Soares
Scott Brewer
Tom Renedo
Traci Hultzapple
Troi Hayes

NFL FEVER 2002

ALL TEAMS AND STADIUMS

Create a new profile and name it Broadway.

All Teams and Stadiums

Team Select

NHL HITZ 20-02

CHEATS

After selecting your players, you will have a chance to enter codes by changing three icons by pressing the X button, Y button and B button. Use the X button to change the first icon, the Y button for second and the B button for the third. You will then need to press in the direction indicated. For example, to enter the code for 1st to 7 Wins, you would press X three times, Y two times and B three times. Then press Left on the Directional pad.

EFFECT	CHEAT
Input More Codes	3 3 3 Right
Ignore Last Code	0 1 0 Down
1st to 7 Wins	3 2 3 Left
Win Fights for goals	2 0 2 Left
No Crowd	2 1 0 Right
Show Hot Spot	2 0 1 Up
Show Shot Speed	1 0 1 Up
Rain	1 4 1 Left
Snow	1 2 1 Left

Snow

Big Puck	1 2 1 Up
Huge Puck	3 2 1 Up

Huge Puck

Bulldozer Puck	2 1 2 Left
Hockey Ball	1 3 3 Left
Tennis Ball	1 3 2 Down
No Puck Out of Play	1 1 1 Down
Big Head Player	2 0 0 Right

EFFECT	CHEAT
Huge Head Player	3 0 0 Right
Big Head Team	2 2 0 Left
Huge Head Team	3 3 0 Left
Always Big Hits	2 3 4 Down
Late Hits	3 2 1 Down
Pinball Boards	4 2 3 Right

Big Head Team

Domino Effect	0 1 2 Right
Turbo Boost	0 0 2 Up

Domino Effect

191

Continued

EFFECT	CHEAT
Infinite Turbo	4 1 3 Right

No Crowd

No Fake Shots	4 2 4 Down
No One-Timers	2 1 3 Left
Skills Versus	2 2 2 Down
Hitz Time	1 0 4 Right

PROJECT GOTHAM RACING

ALL CARS AND COURSES

Enter your name as Nosliw.

Select Screen

All Cars and Courses

STAR WARS: STARFIGHTER SPECIAL EDITION

UNLOCK EVERYTHING
Enter OVERSEER as a code.

INVINCIBILITY
Enter MINIME as a code.

DISABLE HUD
Enter NOHUD as a code.

EXPERIMENTAL N-1 FIGHTER
Enter BLUENSF as a code.

REVERSE CONTROLS
Enter JARJAR as a code.

MULTIPLAYER LEVELS
Enter ANDREW as a code.

DIRECTOR MODE
Enter DIRECTOR as a code.

SHIP GALLERY
Enter SHIPS as a code.

CONCEPT ART
Enter PLANETS as a code.

CHRISTMAS MOVIE
Enter WOZ as a code.

CAST PICTURES
Enter HEROES as a code.

VIEW PROGRAMMING TEAM
Enter TEAM as a code.

JAMES' DAY AT WORK
Enter JAMES as a code.

SIMON PICTURES
Enter SIMON as a code.

VIEW CREDITS
Enter CREDITS as a code.

MESSAGE
Enter LTDJGD as a code.

DEFAULT SCREEN
Enter SIZZLE as a code.

TONY HAWK'S PRO SKATER 2X

ALL CHEATS

Pause the game, hold the Left Trigger and enter SATURDAY BABY, where T is the white button. The screen will shake if entered correctly.

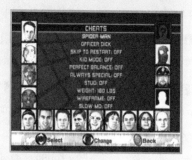

All Cheats

TRANSWORLD SURF

NO HUD

Press Back, Up, Down, Left, Right, Up, Right.

LEGAL

DREAMCAST®

LEGAL

GAME BOY® ADVANCE

Game Boy® Advance is a registered trademark of Nintendo of America Inc.

ARMY MEN ADVANCE © 2001 The 3DO Company All rights reserved.

ATLANTIS: THE LOST EMPIRE © 2001 Disney.

BACKTRACK © 2001 Telegames, Inc. Under License from JV Games, Inc.

BATMAN VENGEANCE © 2001 UBI SOFT Entertainment

BOXING FEVER is a trademark of Digital Fiction Inc. © 2001 Digital Fiction Inc. All rights reserved.

CASTLEVANIA: CIRCLE OF THE MOON © 1986, 2001 KONAMI & KCE Tokyo All Rights Reserved.

EARTHWORM JIM © 2001 Interplay Entertainment Corp. All rights reserved.

F-14 TOMCAT © 2001 MAJESCO, INC.

FIREPRO WRESTLING © 2001 Spike

GRADIUS GALAXIES is a trademark of KONAMI CORPORATION. © 1985 2001 KONAMI & Mobile21 Co., Ltd. ALL RIGHTS RESERVED.

GT ADVANCE CHAMPIONSHIP RACING – Game & Software © 2001 MTO Inc. Exclusively licensed to & distributed by THQ Inc.

IRIDION 3D is a registered trademark of Majesco Sales, Inc. All rights reserved. © 2001 Majesco Sales, Inc.

JURASSIC PARK 3: PARK BUILDER Jurassic Park III is a trademark and copyright of Universal Studios and Amblin Entertainment, Inc. Licensed by Universal Studios Licensing, Inc. All rights reserved. The copyright to the code used to create this electronic videogame belongs to Konami Corporation. ©2001 KONAMI

LEGO BIONICLE: TALES OF THE TOHUNGA ©2001 The Lego Group. ®Lego is a trademark of the lego group. Developed by Saffire Corporation.

MEN IN BLACK: THE SERIES Game Design and Program © 2001 Crave Entertainment, Inc. All Rights Reserved. Men In Black: The Series © 2001 Columbia Pictures Industries, Inc. & Adelaide Productions, Inc.

LEGAL

GAME BOY® COLOR

Game Boy® Color is a registered trademark of Nintendo of America Inc.

102 DALMATIONS: PUPPIES TO THE RESCUE developed by Disney Interactive/Crystal Dynamics/Digital Eclipse, published by Activision. All rights reserved.

ACTION MAN ©2001 Infogrames Interactive, Inc. All Rights Reserved Used With Permission ©2001 THQ Inc. All Rights Reserved.

ARMY MEN 2 ©2001 The 3DO Company All rights reserved.

ARMY MEN: AIR COMBAT ©2001 The 3DO Company All rights reserved.

ARMY MEN: SARGE'S HEROES 2 ©2001 The 3DO Company All rights reserved. .

BLADE developed by HAL Corp. and Avit Inc., published by Activision. All rights reserved.

BUFFY THE VAMPIRE SLAYER © 2000 Twentieth Century Fox Film Corporation. All Rights Reserved. Published and distributed by THQ Inc. © 2000 THQ Inc. All Rights Reserved.

CHICKEN RUN © 2000 THQ Inc. All Rights Reserved.

DAVE MIRRA FREESTYLE BMX™ Developed By Z-Axis. Acclaim ®, Dave Mirra Freestyle Bmx™ And Acclaim Max Sports ™ & ©2000 Acclaim Entertainment, Inc. All Rights Reserved

DEXTER'S LABORATORY: ROBOT RAMPAGE © 2001 BAM! Entertainment. DEXTER'S LABORATORY is a trademark of Cartoon Network © 2000.

DONALD DUCK: GOIN' QUACKERS developed and published by Ubi Soft. All rights reserved.

DRIVER ©2000 Infogrames Entertainment S.A. All Rights Reserved.

INSPECTOR GADGET © 2001 Ubi Soft

JEREMY MCGRATH SUPERCROSS 2000 © 2000 Acclaim Entertainment, Inc.

M&M'S MINIS MADNESS © 2000 Majesco Sales, Inc. All rights reserved.

MAT HOFFMAN'S PRO BMX © 2001 Activision Inc. and its affiliates. All rights reserved.

MEN IN BLACK: THE SERIES 2 ™ © 2000 Columbia Pictures Industries, Inc. & Adelaide Productions, Inc. All rights reserved. Published by Crave Entertainment, Inc. © 2000 Crave Entertainment, Inc.

MEN IN BLACK: THE SERIES™ 2 ©2000 Columbia Pictures Industries, Inc. & Adelaide Productions, Inc. All rights reserved. Trademark: MEN IN BLACK™ Columbia Pictures Industries, Inc. Published by Crave Entertainment, Inc. ©2000 Crave Entertainment, Inc.

MONSTERS INC. © 2001 Disney/Pixar THQ and its logo are trademarks and/or registered trademarks of THQ Inc. All Rights Reserved.

MTV SPORTS: T.J. LAVIN'S ULTIMATE BMX MTV Game and Software © 2000 THQ Inc. "MTV Sports" names, trademarks, and logos and all related titles and logos are trademarks of MTV Networks, a division of Viacom International Inc. All rights reserved.

THE MUMMY RETURNS © 2001 Universal Interactive Studios

NEW ADVENTURES OF MARY KATE AND ASHLEY developed by Crawfish International, published by Acclaim. All rights reserved.

PORTAL RUNNER © 2001 The 3DO Company. All rights reserved.

POWERPUFF GIRLS: BAD MOJO JOJO THE POWERPUFF GIRLS and all related characters and elements are trademarks of Cartoon Network © 2000. Sennari © 2000

POWERPUFF GIRLS: BATTLE HIM published by BAM! Entertainment. All rights reserved.

POWERPUFF GIRLS: PAINT THE TOWNSVILLE GREEN published by BAM! Entertainment. All rights reserved.

POWER RANGERS: TIME FORCE © 2001 THQ, Inc. TM and © 2001 Saban. Power Rangers Time Force and all related logos, characters, names and distinctive likenesses thereof are the exclusive property of Saban Entertainment, Inc and Saban International N.V. All Rights Reserved. ™ & © 2001 Fox/Fox Kids. All Rights Reserved.

LEGAL

LEGAL

GAMECUBE™

LEGAL

NINTENDO 64®

PLAYSTATION®

LEGAL

PLAYSTATION® 2

PlayStation® 2 is a registered trademark of Sony Computer Entertainment Inc. PlayStation and the PlayStation 2 logos are registered trademarks of Sony Computer Entertainment Inc.

4X4 EVOLUTION © 2001 Terminal Reality, Inc.

ARCTIC THUNDER © 2001 Midway Home Entertainment Inc.

ARMY MEN: AIR ATTACK™ 2 © 2001 The 3DO Company. All rights reserved.

ARMY MEN: SARGE'S HEROES 2 © 2000 The 3DO Company. All rights reserved.

ATV OFFROAD FURY © 2001 Sony Computer Entertainment America Inc. Developed by Rainbow Studios.

BATMAN VENGEANCE © 2001 Ubi Soft Entertainment is a trademark of Ubi Soft Inc. Ubi Soft and the Ubi Soft Entertainment logo are registered trademarks of Ubi Soft Inc. All rights reserved. BATMAN and all related characters, names and indicia are trademarks of DC Comics © 2001.

CART FURY © 2001 Midway Home Entertainment Inc.

CRAZY TAXI™ Created by and Produced by SEGA. Converted, Published and distributed by Acclaim. © SEGA 1999, 2000. SEGA and CRAZY TAXI are registered trademarks or trademarks of Sega Corporation. Acclaim® & © 2001 Acclaim Entertainment, Inc. All rights reserved.

DAVE MIRRA FREESTYLE BMX 2 © 2001 Acclaim Entertainment, Inc. All rights reserved.

GAUNTLET: DARK LEGACY © 1998-2000 Midway Games West, Inc. All rights reserved.

GRAND THEFT AUTO III ©2001 All rights reserved. Grand Theft Auto is a trademark of Take Two Interactive Software Inc.

HALF-LIFE © 2001 Sierra Entertainment, Inc. All rights reserved.

KINETICA is a trademark of Sony Computer Entertainment America Inc. © 2001 Sony Computer Entertainment America Inc.

LEGAL

LEGAL

LEGAL

XBOX™